The SAHAR of ZANZIBAR

for Ramona,

Shirley

Shirley Gould

Trilogy Christian Publishers
A Wholly Owned Subsidary of Trinity Broadcasting Network
2442 Michelle Drive
Tustin, CA 92780

For information, address Trilogy Christian Publishing
Rights Department, 2442 Michelle Drive, Tustin, Ca 92780.
Trilogy Christian Publishing/ TBN and colophon are trademarks of Trinity Broadcasting Network.

For information about special discounts for bulk purchases, please contact Trilogy Christian Publishing.

Manufactured in the United States of America

10 9 8 7 6 5 4 3 2 1

Library of Congress Cataloging-in-Publication Data is available.

ISBN 978-1-64773-833-4 (Print Book)
ISBN 978-1-64773-834-1 (ebook)

Shirley not only brings Africa to life but immerses you in a world of both beauty and peril. A gripping story about justice, truth, and the cost of standing up for what you believe in.
—*USA Today*'s best-selling author Susan May Warren

To JR

Our forty years together were filled with saucy romance,
amazing African adventures,
and a plethora of cherished memories.
We faced our challenges as a team
with the Lord as our guide.

Now, as I pen snippets of our story,
it's easy to create a great hero—
because you were my knight in shining Land Rover.

ACKNOWLEDGMENTS

I love this story, and I'm excited to share it with you. But this novel wouldn't be in your hands without the many wonderful people who helped on this journey.

Susan May Warren of Novel Academy has poured writing wisdom into my brain for years—along with her team of stellar authors, Rachel Hauck, Lisa Jordan, Tari Faris, Alena Tauriainen, and Beth Vogt. They got me where I am today, and I'm forever grateful.

Donna Yarborough, my writing partner, has listened to my stories, offered suggestions, and kept me encouraged to keep writing when the road to publication seemed unreachable. I appreciate her faithful friendship.

To my tribe, Shelayne, Sharee, Shontel, Sheri, Johnnie, Jana, Judi, Darlene, Ramona, Carol, and Nina. You have read the many drafts, given input, and prodded me to keep writing. My MBT huddle has encouraged me during the process. Their prayers are so appreciated. Love you, ladies! You make me better!

Thank you!

To my mom and dad, thank you for believing in me and pushing me toward my dreams.

To my wonderful family, you've been so supportive as you've walked this writing journey with me and celebrated my successes. "Thank you" seems inadequate to express my gratitude. To my grands, you give me seven reasons to smile—Madi, Jake, Finley, Charlotte, Judah, Blakely, and Lyda. I love you always. ShoSho.

Rhett Harwell and the wonderful staff at Trilogy Christian Publishing have been amazing to work with. I appreciate their diligence to make this novel the best it could be.

Jeffrey James Torres, my editor, is so talented. He has labored to polish my prose to make it shine. You're amazing. And I'd be remiss not to mention Cornerstone Creative Solutions, who created this stunning cover. Thanks. It's perfect! I want to express special thanks to Christy Phillippe for being my liaison with the production company through every step of this process. I'm eternally grateful.

Finally, I thank the Lord Jesus for walking with me day by day, spurring my creativity. I'm honored by Your call upon my life to touch people through song, teaching, preaching, and now through written words. I'm humbled by Your love for me.

PROLOGUE

The heavy metal gates of the mission compound clanged behind her as Joy Deckland wove her Subaru minivan into Zanzibar's bustling traffic flow.

"Jessicah, when we get to the market, buy a tray of eggs and put them in the van. Then get some onions and tomatoes for tomorrow's meal."

"Sawa, Mama Joy. I will do it."

Joy laid on her horn in an attempt to get a herd of mooing milk makers to clear the dirt road. When they parted, she downshifted and gunned it through the mayhem.

"I'll leave the side door unlocked for your purchases."

"Sawa, Mama. Is it potato day?"

"Yes. The shipment arrived from Tanzania right after lunch. For the best selection, I want to get there before it gets too late in the day. The Zanzibaris will come for their potatoes on their way home from work. I'll get us twenty pounds of potatoes and a large bag of charcoal, then meet you here."

Joy slowed, parked her minivan, and put some shillings into Jessicah's hand. Jessicah smiled at her employer and slipped out of the Subaru.

Joy watched the frail, sweet-spirited woman enter the open market with a smile. Joy pocketed her keys and some money. After swinging her long brown braid to her back, she perched her sunglasses on top of her head. Making a path under a dingy canvas awning that offered a reprieve from the scorching African sun, she moved toward the back of the overgrown kiosk. Joy sauntered through rows of stacked produce, cages of live chickens, and baskets of beans. Reaching the piles of potatoes, she pivoted, searching the area for the Zanzibari woman she usually bought from, who wasn't manning her kiosk. *That's weird. Someone is always here.* She couldn't find a soul. *Something's wrong.*

"Where is everyone?"

"They have taken a dinner break."

That evil voice grated on her last nerve. The hairs rose on the back of her neck as she scanned the market for anyone who could help her—but found the area abandoned. Jessicah was busy at the front row of the market, where the chaos of the evening traffic would drown any cry for help. She turned slowly.

"Aga Kahn, what do you want?" Though petite in stature, Joy perched both hands on her hips and met his intense gaze.

His white robes and turban exuded the power he thought he had as the leader of Islam on the island. "I've warned you many times, but you have failed to listen. Now, I want you silenced!"

"That's not going to happen. I've come to Zanzibar to spend my life sharing hope and love as I spread the good news of Jesus."

He stepped forward. "I demand that you stop!"

"No! This island needs our Christian message." She hid her fear behind a cold stare.

He blew out a hot, angry breath and motioned for his man to come closer.

"You don't scare me, Aga Kahn," she lied.

"As the Sahar of Zanzibar, you are not a wise woman. You've angered me too many times." He stepped closer.

"This conversation is over. I'm reporting you to the police, Kahn." She spun around and started to leave the market.

Kahn's hired man grabbed her. She kicked him, jabbed her elbow into his side, and struggled against his strength for release as he put a cloth over her mouth. The sweet-smelling concoction on the material caused her to relax. Her knees buckled. She tried to scream, to signal for help, but her body wouldn't cooperate. The man carried her out the back of the market and dumped her drugged body in the back of a large black SUV and tied a gag across her mouth.

Dizzy, weak, and disoriented, she tried to make sense of what was happening. He slammed the back door as the truck's engine revved. She felt every pothole as he drove entirely too fast, tossing her back and forth.

Jessicah won't know where I am. If Kahn is trying to scare me, it's working this time. But I refuse to stop doing what I've been sent to do.

Aga Kahn's man hit the brakes, slamming her body against the bench seat. He opened his door, causing the beeping of the ignition to call for attention. As evening traffic sped by, Joy heard his footsteps as he moved to the rear of the SUV and opened the back door.

Joy was ready. She kicked him in the stomach and tried to get out. He took the hit and shoved her back onto the floor of the vehicle, raised a silver blade, and stabbed her twice, turning the knife with the second penetration. Her scream was muffled by the gag as excruciating pain stole her breath. Jerking Joy out of the SUV before her blood stained the carpet, he dropped her in the dirt outside the gate of her mission compound. He kicked her twice on the wounds he had inflicted, then hurried to make his escape. He sped away, slinging dirt and debris on her wounded body as Joy's blood soaked Zanzibar's soil.

As his taillights faded into the distance, Joy held her hands on the wounds with as much force as she could muster.

Cars, buses, and vans passed, emitting clouds of exhaust as they stirred dust in their wake. A dog sniffed her and barked before moving on. Feeling weak from blood loss and pain, she lost consciousness. Coming to again, she tried to cry out as dirt filled her eyes. Using the last of her energy, she kicked the gate, attempting to get the guard's attention. The movement caused blood to gush from her stab wounds.

Lord, I'm sorry I haven't finished the task You sent me to do. Gasping for a breath, she winced against the pain. Blood was filling her mouth. Time was slipping away. *Please take care of Eli and my sweet baby, Judah.*

Though the sun hadn't set in Zanzibar's cerulean sky, everything went black for Joy Deckland.

CHAPTER 1

"Air turbulence can't compete with ocean waves." Olivia Stone held her hair back to lose her lunch over the bow of the old ferry as they neared the coast of Zanzibar. When she attempted to focus on the horizon, the noonday sun glistening on the waves caused her to heave all the more.

"You okay, miss?" An elderly Tanzanian woman leaned close, offering her a couple of tissues.

"I will be when I get my feet on solid ground." She wiped her mouth and moved toward the gangplank with her luggage in tow. Letting pedestrians disembark first before vehicles drove off the ferry allowed Olivia to get off as soon as they reached the wide dock.

Seeking a change in her future, a place to make a difference, she was eager to explore this exotic port. As a flight attendant, she flew the African skies taking passengers to amazing places for adventures. But it was getting routine. As she contemplated a major employment shift, a life change, to live and work somewhere on the continent, Zanzibar seemed like a great place to consider.

As the ferry passengers dispersed, all eyes focused on Olivia, the only white foreigner in a sea of Africans. The slapping of the ferry's wake against the bulkhead caused her stomach to roil in protest. She hurried through the bustling throng toward dry land, bringing her face-to-face with a turbaned Indian ruler who blocked her path.

"Joy Deckland, you were not to return! I demand you depart!" he hissed toward Olivia's ear as he leaned close to her body.

"Back up, Ali Baba, if you don't want me to puke all over your robes." She rushed around him with her suitcase, bumping behind her on the uneven, weathered boardwalk.

"You cannot ignore Aga Kahn!" He was right behind her.

As she stepped on the sand, she turned left. Hurrying to the water's edge, she bent over and lost the last of her lunch.

The enraged Indian paced a few feet away, yelling, "Usama!" into his cell phone.

Olivia wiped her mouth and took a deep breath. She pivoted, searching for the angry man, who had crossed the road, still engrossed in his call. *What's his problem?* "Keep your distance, Buster. I may be petite, but dynamite comes in small packages." *That's telling him, Olivia.*

She blew out a breath and relaxed, perusing Zanzibar for the first time. The beach displayed dirty white sand with a rocky mixture, but thankfully, it wasn't moving. Solid ground. Olivia pulled at the waist of her skinny jeans, straightened her cold-shoulder, floral-print blouse, put her long hair behind her ear, and hoped the humidity hadn't messed with her makeup. With her grip tightened on the raised handle of her suitcase, she smiled, scanning the coastal scene. A change of pace was just the ticket, as this flight attendant became the tourist. *I'll find a place for me, for my future, with my toes in this sand. I'm sure of it.*

The port served as a market place for the locals. Kiosks lined the area with merchandise—clothes to raw meat, charcoal to flashlights, fruit to flip-flops. They offered everything except a cold bottle of water. She put her hand into her pocket and pulled out a cellophane-covered mint and popped it into her mouth.

Among the colorful chaos, dogs scrounged around for a meal, competing with seagulls swooping in to steal their find. Palm trees danced in the ocean breeze as the locals sold to residents in the bustling market. Fish were being tossed to shop owners. Women with babies tied on their backs grilled shrimp kebabs over charcoal. Live roosters with their feet tied together crowed in protest of pending sales. Olivia closed her eyes momentarily and took a deep breath, which made her shudder, as an array of fishy smells assaulted her senses. Her stomach growled a threat.

Amid the throng, Muslim women hidden behind flowing black robes bustled about in the business of buying and selling. Old men struggled to push carts of pineapples, selling them along the road. Pungent body odors rivaled the strong aroma of the juicy fruit. Donkeys brayed in the distance. Straining nets of fresh catch were being off-loaded from old boats tied to the rickety pier. A mixture of languages competed with crashing waves slapping the bulkhead and the cries of ibis circling overhead. Colorful prints of women's attire on this Swahili coast stood out in front of the off-white stucco buildings of Stone Town, definitely a mixture of Africans and Asians vying for a few measly shillings.

"Mama, Mama." A cute little boy ran toward Olivia. His short legs carried him across the sand. He lifted his arms for her to pick him up. "Mama." His white skin and big brown eyes, framed by his reddish-blond hair, singled him out in the crowd of Zanzibaris.

Olivia picked him up, straining at his weight. "Hey, little guy. You're a heavy dude. Where's your mommy and daddy?"

He smiled and patted her cheek. "Mama." He put his arm around her neck and laid his head on her shoulder and kept patting her back. His wrinkled khaki pants had a match-box car in the pocket.

What an adorable child. Olivia rubbed his back as she searched the area. *Someone will be looking for him and probably suspect me of taking the boy.*

"Judah! Where are you? Come to Mama Frances. Judah!" An African woman rushed toward Olivia and stopped short when she saw her cradling him. The woman stood statuesque, with one hand over her mouth, while she held bags of fruits and veggies in the other as a salty breeze fanned her long skirt and apron. Her graying hair was in a tight bun at her nape. Wrinkles around her eyes showed her concern for the boy.

An American man hurried from the market, heading toward their direction, carrying a fish wrapped in newsprint. "Frances, have you found Judah?"

"Ndio, Bwana. Yes. He is here." She pointed to Olivia holding Judah.

He stopped short, sending dust flying around his boots. He grabbed a cart by the road as if to keep from falling. "Joy?" He stared at Olivia as the color drained from his face.

Olivia watched him. He could have stepped off a page of a Bass Pro catalog spread. That type of angler shirt was popular with rugged men, and he fit that category to a tee. "Is this adorable boy your son? I'm not trying to take him. Please believe me. I was seasick on the ferry, so I stayed right here, allowing my stomach to settle. Your son ran to me with his arms up, wanting me to hold him. I hope that's all right. He was getting close to the water…" Olivia watched the man bend over at the waist with his hands on his knees. He took

16

a deep breath and sighed, wiped his perspiring brow, then stood and eased her direction.

"Yes. That's Judah, my son. Who…who are you?" He stood a few feet from her.

"I'm Olivia Stone. I've just got off the ferry for a two-week vacation. I needed a change of scenery. I know a bit of Swahili, so Zanzibar seemed the logical place to explore." She babbled info to fill the uncomfortable silence stalled between them while she rubbed the boy's back as he relaxed in slumber.

"I'm Eli Deckland, a missionary here in Zanzibar. Forgive my hesitation, but you look like my late wife, Joy. Judah must have thought you were her."

"Bless his heart. He must miss his mother. I'm sorry for your loss."

"Thanks, Ms. Stone." Eli moved toward Olivia. "He can get heavy. Let me take him." Eli gave the fish he'd purchased to Mama Frances, then stepped into Olivia's personal space to take his son.

As he reached for the boy, his hand rubbed against her arm, sending a shiver through her. Their eyes met. She sucked in a deep breath and held it as if frozen under the hot tropical sun. Her dry throat got drier. Parched.

"Thanks for being understanding about Judah." He cradled his son, pulling him close.

Olivia eased back a few inches as the breeze sent his woodsy cologne her direction. "No harm done. He just took me by surprise."

"It's a pleasure to meet you, Olivia Stone. I hope you enjoy your stay in Zanzibar." He stepped toward his SUV parked about twenty feet away. Pausing, he turned back and stared at Olivia again while giving direction to his worker. "Frances, let's get Judah home."

Olivia watched as he fastened his son into a car seat while his worker loaded their purchases in the back of the SUV.

Not to be caught staring, Olivia searched for a cab. A hair-raising feeling tightened her gut; she scanned her surroundings, her senses alert. When she locked eyes with the Indian man across the rocky road, he stared daggers her direction. Goose bumps marched down her arms. She hugged herself, then waved for a taxi as smoke from burning trash wafted her direction.

A four-door taxi that had seen better days slowed in front of her. The engine back-fired when he stopped, causing her to jerk slightly.

Inhaling exhaust, she opened the back door. "Ocean Paradise Resort and Spa, Bwana."

She reached for her suitcase but didn't move fast enough. The Indian man grabbed her arm, restricting any movement. Pulling her close, he spoke in hushed, angry tones, his acrid breath making it difficult for her to breathe.

"The Sahar of Zanzibar...have you returned from the grave to haunt me? You will not win. It is perilous for you to be on my island. I warned you before. Hear me now! Leave on the ferry within two days or meet my wrath. Understand?"

Captive in his grasp, she jerked back with wide eyes as he spit his threats. In her peripheral vision, she spied the missionary rushing her direction. "Let me go!" Olivia pulled her arm out of the Indian's grip.

"Olivia, let me give you a ride to your hotel." Eli forced himself between the Indian and Olivia to retrieve her luggage. "We're always glad to have tourists on our island."

Olivia wiped drops of perspiration from her forehead as she followed the missionary. Trembling, she slid into the front seat of his SUV and fumbled her attempts to fasten the seat belt.

Eli watched her, locked the doors, and offered assistance with her seat belt before he plunged them into traffic flow, leaving the angry Indian in the dust. "You okay?"

Olivia saw the Indian in the side mirror as she massaged her arm where he'd grabbed her. "I think I'll have a bruise. But I'm okay." She took some deep breaths in an attempt to get her heart rate back on even keel. "Thanks for coming to my rescue. Ali Baba was furious." Her voice rose to a soprano level as she spoke. She laughed nervously.

"What did he say to you?" He glanced in her direction, then returned his focus on the road.

"He called me the Sahar of Zanzibar and asked if I'd come back from the grave to torment him. He demanded I leave on the ferry within two days or else. Who does he think he is?"

"Ali Baba?" The corner of Eli's mouth lifted in a slight smile.

"Yeah, like Ali Baba and the forty thieves."

"It's almost comical how close you are in your assessment. His name is Aga Kahn. I think he gave himself that title so people would assume he's a relative of His Highness Prince Karim Aga Kahn IV, but there's no relation. He thinks he rules Zanzibar and demands to be treated like royalty. He doesn't want Christianity to spread in this Muslim stronghold."

"Sounds like you've faced him before." She perused the handsome missionary, probably six feet tall, very toned, and tan, truly a commanding presence with a strong jaw and calloused, worker-man hands.

Eli downshifted the Land Rover SUV as they neared a traffic jam. "I have, many times. He's dangerous. Proceed with caution, Ms. Stone."

"Since you rescued me, you can call me Olivia."

He took a detour on the side of the road. "Which resort are you staying at?"

"Ocean Paradise Resort and Spa. You know where it is?"

"Yeah, on a great strip of beach. Good choice." He dodged a goat meandering across the road and stole a look at her. "You don't have a twin, do you?"

"No, I'm an only child. Why?" She caught a look at his profile. *Are all rescuers this good-looking? Clean cut, well-built, with amber eyes.* His brown hair had just enough curl to rebel against being styled. Too bad he was a grieving widower and a missionary on assignment. He could put her heart in a tug-of-war. *I'm a Christian, but missionary work takes commitment to a whole other level. So nix that idea, Olivia.*

He downshifted the SUV as they circled a roundabout. "You're a replica of my wife, until I hear your voice or look into your eyes."

"No wonder you looked as if you'd seen a ghost. I've read there are six degrees of separation and everyone has a twin somewhere, but there is a minute chance you'd ever meet them." Her nervousness had her chatting excessively. *Maybe I'm more upset than I thought.* She braced herself for a pothole in the tarmac. "You think that's why Aga Kahn said I'd returned from the grave to torment him, don't you?"

He didn't answer.

She watched the scene of the locals laboring and children playing with handmade toys. "He called me a Sahar. What's a Sahar?"

"*Sahar* has several meanings. It's that special moment just before dawn. A *Sahar* is also a special person who is known to be enchanting, gifted, and happy. She's called a falcon."

"A falcon flying over Africa—I'm a flight attendant who flies the African skies. But how would he know that?"

He hesitated again. "He probably doesn't. He thinks you're my late wife. *Sahar* also refers to a finder of truth. Which is probably the meaning he was using."

"I don't understand."

He pulled the truck into the entrance of Ocean Paradise Resort and put it in park then faced Olivia. "My wife was overly bold in her witnessing. She loved to 'share the truth of the gospel' to anyone who would listen. Many Muslims have converted to Christianity because of Joy. She angered Aga Kahn repeatedly, and after several warnings, she was stabbed and left bleeding at my gate. Twenty-four hours later, she died."

Tears filled Olivia's eyes. "That had to be devastating. Why are you still here?"

"I can't leave until I prove who took Joy's life. I owe her that much. I've been gathering clues for a year but can't prove it yet. It's like I'm chasing the wind. My replacement on this mission assignment is in language school, learning Swahili as we speak, so my time left here is limited."

"I understand. Is Judah at risk?" She glanced back at the sleeping child.

"I thought he could have been taken today, then I saw you."

"Tough afternoon. Sorry." She started to touch his arm, then pulled back.

"Just be careful, Olivia."

He took her phone and put his number in it and called his phone to capture her number. "Call if you need anything. I'll text you my address. Zanzibar is an amazing place, but it can be dangerous for a woman traveling alone." He got out and retrieved her suitcase from the back of the SUV.

The touch of his hand as she took her luggage sent warmth up her arm. She met his eyes and bit her bottom lip. Staring for a long moment, she held his gaze. "I'm sorry for your pain, Eli. You be careful. You've got some precious cargo in that car seat." She rolled her bag toward the registration desk but looked back once more. He was still where she'd left him. "Thanks for the ride."

He lifted his hand in a wave and turned to leave.

Olivia waited in line at the reception desk while contemplating her strange afternoon. It was a weird day. A little boy thought she was his mother, then she was threatened by a terrorist and rescued by a hero. All she wanted was to explore her options about a future on this island, not to come face-to-face with the man of her dreams with mesmerizing eyes. She was not looking for romance, like in those fairy-tale novels that passengers leave on airplanes. She needed sand and sun, and some peace and quiet, then several job interviews. Now she was in the middle of drama, drama, drama. What was it about her that brought out the crazies?

*****

Aga Kahn perched his hands on his hips and watched the American's vehicle speed away. If his piercing gaze obeyed the wishes of his mind, the Sahar would have turned to salt on the spot. *She should have stayed dead. Now she must experience my wrath again.* Dust billowed at Aga Kahn's feet as the missionary drove away. *Doesn't their Bible say ashes to ashes and dust to dust? They need a stern reminder.*

Aga Kahn pulled out his cell phone and spoke loudly, competing with the traffic noise. "Fahad, meet me at my office in ten minutes. Bring Zubair with you. We have a problem."

He texted his driver, slammed the phone shut, then put it in the hidden pocket of his robe. Within minutes, his luxury sedan pulled to the side of the road. The driver hurried to open the door for him before returning to the driver's seat.

"To my home office, Asim." Aga Kahn plotted possibilities during the drive. The streets, bustling with people, animals, and vehicles, hindered their progress, irritating him all the more.

When his building came into view, he admired the arched entry with his ornate door. When the Sahar was off Zanzibar Island, he planned to add additional adornments to his door. People needed to be reminded of his importance.

Fahad opened his door for him when he arrived. "Zubair will be here within five minutes."

"Good. Have my chefs prepare masala tea and serve it in the conference room. Tell them to bring nans or bread. And hurry. I'll be waiting." Aga Kahn allowed his houseworker to dust the edge of his robe and his sandaled feet before he stomped into the building. He paced the conference room several times before he took his seat at the head of the lacquered table and banged his fist on its surface. Breathing deep several times, he replayed the encounter at the port.

With a furrowed brow and clenched jaw, he stared at one of the ornate chandeliers that hung over the gleaming table hosting twenty high-back chairs. Persian rugs to cushion their steps were made in burgundy and deep-blue designs that matched the velvet of the ornate seats. But the grandeur of the room didn't temper Aga Kahn's anger at this recent turn of events.

Zubair apologized for being late. "I came with haste, Aga Kahn. Sorry for your distress."

"Have tea." Aga Kahn motioned for them to be seated, then sipped his brew. Fahad and Zubair drank their tea and ate a nan until the moment Aga Kahn finished his drink. Then teatime had ended.

Kahn stood and paced. "When I give an order, I expect it to be carried out as I have instructed. Without exception. When it doesn't happen, I get angry. Very angry." He stared at the wide-eyed men.

"I must inform you that Joy Deckland lives. I spoke with her today. She arrived from Dar es Salaam on the ferry this afternoon. I commanded Usama to end her life. But he failed me. What do you know of this?" He looked from one man to the other. "I called him, but his phone went directly to voice mail."

Fahad stood to speak. "Aga Kahn, I know he stabbed her and left her body at the missionary's gate. When Deckland found her, he took her to the hospital. I heard the guard at his compound say she died the next day, but I do not have proof of her demise." Fahad took his seat.

Zubair stood. "The missionary and his small son went to the mainland the next day to take her body to the United States. Could she have lived and they are deceiving us?" Zubair sat again.

"I do not know, but her return infuriates me. Usama's name means lion, but he didn't complete the job as I instructed. Is he a coward? A liar? I want you men to question him. We will have to deal with his failure. Zubair, check with your contacts at the hospital. Confirm her death. Fahad, get me a copy of Joy Deckland's photo from the Visa Office. I told the Sahar to leave Zanzibar. If she isn't on the ferry when it departs within two days, we will take extreme measures. I will watch her tonight and tomorrow night if she risks staying on the island. Be back at this same time tomorrow. We may have to make strategic plans to clean up Usama's mess."

The two men stood and bowed before backing out of the conference room on quiet feet. Aga Kahn lifted a bell and rang it. A servant entered. "Yes, Bwana."

"I am stressed. Prepare some entertainment for me. Are the dancers here?"

"Yes, Bwana. I will summon them. Should I dismiss your driver for the day?" The worker was careful not to make eye contact.

"No. I'll be going out again."

"I will inform him, Bwana." He bowed and backed out of the room.

Aga Kahn drank another cup of his inky brew as he contemplated the fate of the Sahar. *Death will come swiftly for her this time. I keep my promises.*

*****

Judah slept while Frances hummed an old worship song that had been written by Africans, "God Is so Good," as Eli maneuvered the afternoon traffic with its stops and starts and near misses. He'd had too many conflicting emotions for one afternoon. His heart had skipped a beat when Frances yelled at him across the market.

"Bwana, I cannot find Judah!"

Panic gripped him as he searched for his little boy, the only bright spot in his life. He'd checked the area where they sold live chickens. But no Judah. He looked under the tables, hide-and-seek—his favorite game—but no Judah. He stood on some crates, elevating himself to scan the area. But no Judah. *Has he been kidnapped? O God, please no!* He hurried toward the water, a parent's worst fear pushing him forward.

Then he saw Frances—and Judah—in *Joy's* arms and nearly fainted.

Frances hadn't moved, apparently shocked to see Olivia holding Judah. She waited quietly and allowed Eli to handle the situation.

It pained him to relive the experience.

"Bwana, my heart beat so fast when I couldn't find baby Judah." Frances spoke quietly so Judah wouldn't wake up. "I searched and searched. When my eyes found our boy in her arms, I thought Mama Joy had returned to us. But she does not speak like Mama Joy. Did the Lord send her?"

Oh, I couldn't be that lucky. "I don't know, but God is faithful and has seen our tears. Maybe the Lord sent her for Judah. He's sleeping so peacefully now."

Frances checked on the boy. "This is the first time he isn't crying while sleeping like he usually does."

When they arrived at the missionary compound, Eli waited for the guard to open their gate. "I hope it gave him peace, Frances. Losing his mother has been rough on him." Eli parked the SUV in front of their mission house made of cement blocks, metal doors, and a tin roof. Not an attractive dwelling, but large enough and very secure. He carried Judah to his bed to finish his nap. Before leaving the room, Eli moved the boy's hair off his forehead and kissed him. *I hope it helped you, little buddy, because it devastated me.*

While Frances prepared dinner, Eli got comfortable on the sofa, as comfortable as you can on a futon. He took off his boots and ran his fingers through his unruly hair. His mind replayed his afternoon, especially the moment he saw Olivia. The shock stole his breath. Their similarities in size and long hair. She stood like Joy, all the way down to her skinny jeans and boots. But Olivia's voice was kind, her temperament sweet and caring. Her eyes were chocolate, rich dark chocolate. Her compassion for his loss touched his heart. Not one of Joy's characteristics. Joy had her strengths, her passion for the lost, her knowledge of the Word, and her prayer life. She was frugal yet given to hospitality. Her strong veneer could be misinterpreted as harsh, but her loving way with Judah showed her tender side.

What was he doing? Listing the pros and cons of the attributes of two women who could pass for twins wasn't a good idea. Mixed emotions caused questions. *Lord, I know You orchestrate our lives, and I trust You. But are You playing with my heart? Who's Olivia Stone? Do her looks put her in danger? What will this do to Judah? Will seeing Olivia increase his struggle to sleep? I need to protect him. And Your Word says for me to guard my heart. I'm trying, but I've been consumed from the first moment I laid eyes on Olivia. Is it Joy's looks or her sweet spirit that stirs my emotions, that draws me? Please help me navigate these deep waters. I might drown this time.*

CHAPTER 2

"Paradise is a perfect name for this place." Olivia stood on polished stone floors as she surveyed the massive thatched roof over the reception area. Bouquets of bird-of-paradise flowers were strategically placed in the lobby among the rattan furniture with tropical-print-covered cushions. She'd love to touch those flowers, but it might be frowned upon.

"So glad you approve, Ms. Stone. I'm Mary Emani. I hope you enjoy your time with us. Your oceanfront room is down the hallway to the right. It's a long walk, but the view is breathtaking."

Olivia accepted the key and checked the room out, and it didn't disappoint. Her suite was the perfect setting for a romance novel. A large wall of windows framed a seascape of white sand, swaying palm trees, and ocean waves. The bed was encircled by a satin-edged mosquito net, and a display of fuchsia bougainvillea stood placed on the vanity. Towels were folded in the shape of a swan, welcoming her to Zanzibar. Chilled pineapple juice and stemware waited to refresh her. Perfect for a weary traveler in jet lag.

She poured a glass and enjoyed the sweet nectar while she rubbed the satin on the mosquito net. After donning a sundress and some sandals, she secured her valuables in the safe and grabbed her sunglasses and the book she'd started reading on the plane. Exploring the grounds and watching an African sunset sounded enjoyable after her eventful afternoon.

"Is your room to your liking?" Loy Makua, the hotel manager, asked as she strolled through the lobby.

"Oh yes, it's perfect." She stopped to smell the bouquet of roses on the counter.

"Please take one of the roses, Ms. Stone. Let us know how we can make your stay more pleasurable."

She thanked him, pulled a bloom from the bouquet, and made her way to the beach. At the edge of the sand, she closed her eyes and let the breeze wash over her. The salty air lifted her hair off her perspiring skin. After she removed her shoes, powdery sand oozed between her toes while cool water crept closer with every wave, threatening high tide that would consume this stretch of beach soon. Standing at the water's edge, she watched a sailboat gliding on the horizon in front of a deep-blue sky. Dark clouds in the distance threatened a storm.

Moving back toward the resort, she got comfortable in a lounge chair under a thatched umbrella and let the events of her busy morning ease away. Relaxing, reading, and a short nap were a great plan for a pleasant afternoon, if she could get a sweet little boy out of her mind. He thought she was his mother. How sad. Olivia watched the waves coming and going in repetitive rhythm, allowing her thoughts of the child to linger. Which was better, she wondered, not being able to have children, like herself, or to have a precious child like Judah and leave him motherless? Sometimes there aren't answers but, life keeps going, like the waves slapping the sand over and over.

She opened her book and tried to remember where she'd stopped reading. She was thumbing through the pages when her eyes stopped on the words "He grabbed her," which took her back to the angry Indian she'd encountered at the port. It sent shivers down her spine. She took a deep breath and tried to shake off its lingering effects. It was probably a scary case of mistaken identity. But he didn't follow them. She could see him watching their exit in the rearview mirror. *Glad that's over.*

A waiter walked her direction. "Can I get a soft drink, Bwana?" She needed something refreshing to help her move past those bad vibes.

"Yes. We have Coke and Sprite today." He waited.

"Coke is great."

He hurried to serve her.

Squeals of children entering the cool waves made Olivia smile. Their laughter sent the gulls into flight, but they soon returned to steal chips that the kids dropped as they played.

Her waiter used a bottle opener to open her Coke. She held her glass of purified ice as he poured the soda, thanked him, and took a long drink. Drops of condensation formed quickly under the tropical sun.

Finding her place in her book, she read several pages until the author described how the touch of the hero's hand affected the heroine, transporting Olivia to the moment Eli reached for Judah. His touch sent warmth through her body. As they stood face-to-face, she could see the tiniest touches of gold in his amber eyes. As their gazes locked, she felt a connection with the handsome missionary. Did he feel it too, or was he looking for differences between her and his late wife? Joy gave him Judah; she was a whole person, not like Olivia. Was he thinking about her when he stared at Olivia? That was probably it, she figured. He was still grieving. But when she was in trouble, Eli had come to her rescue, making him her hero, a valiant knight in a shining Land Rover.

She enjoyed a nap, stretched, and read several chapters in her novel. As the afternoon faded, her thoughts returned to Eli. She removed the rose petals off the stem one by one, feeling the softness and savoring their fragrance as she removed each petal sort of like the "he loves me, he loves me not" game she played as a girl. Relationships are complicated, and this would never work. It would be wise to keep him in the friend category. She'd be gone in two weeks, and he'd be here in Zanzibar, unless she found a job on this island. He'd said something about his time at this missionary post coming to an end. They were moving in opposite directions. She decided to enjoy her time on the island without getting her emotions entangled.

As she stepped into the dining room, the smell of fresh-baked bread and steak being grilled wafted her direction. Her stomach growled. Losing her lunch in the Indian Ocean left her with quite an appetite.

"Ready for dinner, Ms. Stone? Your table is prepared. Follow me." The manager turned and led her to a linen-covered table complete with candlelight and flowers.

"Thank you, Bwana Makua. I haven't eaten since lunch in Dar es Salaam. This is lovely."

"Your soup will be served first, then help yourself to the buffet. We have a variety of dishes to please our diverse clientele. Enjoy your dinner!" He bowed, then left her table.

After a bowl of oxtail soup, she gave the waiter her drink order and visited the grill for a piece of steak. As she held her plate for the chef to serve a cut of meat, she caught a glimpse of a man in white robes near a large column. *No! Not again.* Surely, other Indian men dressed in robes like that in Zanzibar.

At her table, the waiter served her drink. After surveying the restaurant for Ali Baba, not seeing him, she relaxed and enjoyed the wonderful food. Tourists from several corners of the world surrounded her. An array of languages and clothing styles made it entertaining to people-watch. Loud American children competed with uncontrollable Indian offspring to see who could exhaust their nanny the fastest.

A bush baby caused quite a stir as he climbed the rafters of the restaurant. Olivia watched the furry nocturnal animal creep higher, away from the sound of silverware hitting china and noisy children demanding attention.

Her waiter brought her another soft drink.

"Is the bush baby tame, Bwana?" Olivia watched the quiet animal climb higher.

"No, they are very shy. There are two of them. Look, the second one is following her mate. Some Americans named them George and Barbara. They come out at night and watch our guests. We leave food for them when we close each evening."

Olivia tried to take a photo, but they were too far away and candlelight made the restaurant too dim.

After ordering hot tea and flan for dessert, she checked her phone for messages from her friends Ellie and Jocelyn. When she looked up, she saw him. Aga Kahn stared at her from across the restaurant with his fists clenched as the brisk evening breeze blew his robes. Her breath caught. Her hand shook. *He doesn't give up, does he?*

The waiter served her tea.

"Bwana, who is the man in the white robes? Does he work here?" She poured sugar into the cup.

He looked at the Indian man. "I have not seen him. He is not employed at Ocean Paradise."

"Please ask the manager about him. He is making me nervous." She held both hands around her warm cup.

"I will right away." He hurried to speak to his boss.

Olivia's cell rang in her hand. She jumped, startled by the ring. She answered the unknown number. "Hello."

"Olivia, this is Eli Deckland. I've seen some of Aga Kahn's men watching my house and wanted to make sure you were okay." He sounded nervous, rushed his words.

"I had a wonderful afternoon until Ali Baba showed up during dinner."

"Did he threaten you again?" Eli's voice intensified.

She looked up to find the Indian staring at her. "No, he has kept his distance. I think he just wants me to know he's watching. But it makes me edgy."

"Is your room secure?"

"Yes. There are good locks on the windows and doors." She took a sip of her tea.

"Don't walk there alone. Have an employee go with you. Then call me, okay?"

"I don't want to keep bothering you, Eli." She cut into her flan.

"You didn't create this problem. I'll be up for a few hours. Call me when you're securely in your room."

"Will do." She ended the call and finished her dessert.

The manager made his way to her table. "The Indian gentleman said he was here on business. He's not staying at the resort."

"He stared at me during dinner, making me uneasy. I think I'd like to go to my room. Can an employee walk with me?"

"I will be glad to accompany you to your quarters, Ms. Stone. Would you like more tea before you retire for the evening?"

"No, I'm good." She stood, left a tip on the table, and followed him down the long dark hall.

Looking authoritative in his suit and tie, Manager Makau led the way. "I hope you enjoyed your afternoon."

"I did. The resort is amazing, and your staff is efficient and kind. A couple of days relaxing on this beach will be a true vacation. Thank you for escorting me, Bwana."

He took her key from her hand, opened the door, and stepped aside for her to enter. "Sleep well, Ms. Stone."

"Thanks." Once the door was closed, Olivia changed quickly, closed the mosquito net around the bed, lifted one side, and slipped between the sheets. With a cell phone in hand, she smiled and pressed Eli's number.

"Hello," he answered in a hushed voice.

"Did I wake you?"

He took a minute to answer. "No. I was checking on Judah and didn't want to wake him. Are you in your room?"

"Yes. The manager was my escort. I'm safe and sound." She fluffed her pillows and reached for the book she was reading on the beach.

"Thanks for letting me know. I feel responsible for your troubles today with Aga Kahn."

"I appreciate your concern for my safety. I'm locked up, safe and sound for tonight. I plan to lie on the beach, soak up some sun, and watch the waves come in and out. I'll be with other guests at the resort. You do your missionary thing. This place is safe."

"Okay. Sounds like you're going to enjoy our beautiful seascape. Rest well, Olivia."

"You too." She ended the call, but her thoughts stayed on Eli. A man of integrity willing to sacrifice for others to know the Lord. His strong, clean-cut look, his concern for her safety, and his love for his son put Eli head and shoulders above any man she'd ever met. His tender touch sent warmth through her even as she relived the moment. *How long do men wait after their wife passes before they open their hearts to love again?* What was she thinking? He was probably thinking about his late wife when he looked at her face. *I don't want to be a replacement.* She chided herself and buried her wayward thoughts in her novel until her eyes grew heavy.

*****

After checking on Judah once more, Eli got busy with his studies for Sunday's sermon. Nightly noises of nocturnal animals became a sound machine that tuned out the chaos of Zanzibar as he focused. With a special message burning on his heart, he researched biblical examples to use to bring his point home to his congregation.

Frances knocked on his door. "Bwana, Jessicah is in much pain. Could we call the doctor?" Frances was jostling Jessicah's baby, Becca, who was unhappy.

Eli rose from his desk. "Yes, give me Becca and her bottle and call the doctor. Is it her heart?"

"Yes. She said her chest is hurting, and her arm." She went to the phone table and made the call.

Eli got comfortable in the living room of his modest home and fed Becca her bottle. Jessicah had health issues with her heart when Joy hired her as house help, but having Becca had taken its toll.

"Bwana, the doctor is coming. Do you want me to take the baby?" She stepped closer.

"I can feed her and get her to sleep if you can stay by Jessicah. Tell her I'm praying for her. I know she's struggling." He took the bottle out of Becca's mouth and put her on his shoulder to burp her. "Frances, ask the doctor if there's anything we can do to make Jessicah more comfortable."

"I will." She left to help her friend, Becca's dying mother.

Eli laid Becca in his arms again and let her finish her bottle. He gazed at her light-brown skin, perfect pink lips, and beautiful blue eyes. "Sweet baby girl, your mother is going to heaven soon. But don't worry, if the good Lord blesses my plan, I'll take care of you."

She watched Eli, not understanding his words but seeming comfortable in his embrace as sleep weighted her eyes.

Eli prayed for Becca and her mother while the doctor attended to his patient. Divine intervention would be appreciated as their futures hung in the balance.

*****

Sounds of workers sweeping the sidewalks woke Olivia. The call of ibis flying overhead entertained her as she dressed. A gauzy sundress over a swimming suit was her choice for this day of leisure. After a breakfast of fresh fruit, eggs, and bacon, she got comfortable in a lounge chair under a thatched umbrella.

"Mama, you buy from me so I can feed my babies?" A Zanzibari woman in bright, mismatched clothes was peddling an armload of kikois, pieces of cloth in African prints.

"Bei gani, how much?" Olivia sat forward and asked for her price.

The woman gave her a fair price, so she chose three pieces, one for herself and one for her two best friends, Jocelyn and Ellie. Olivia gave her the money, took off her sundress, and tied the kikoi around her, using it as a cover-up. The Zanzibari woman smiled before moving on to other customers.

Olivia's cell phone rang as she grabbed her novel. "Hello."

"Hi, Liv. It's Ellie."

Olivia smiled. "It's the wee hours of the morning there. Why are you still up?"

"Jet lag. I did the Australia route. They were short a flight attendant, and the extra money will pad my savings account. Liv, I'm curious. You like Zanzibar?"

"It's an exotic island, a piece of paradise. I'm enjoying the beach today, and I'll start seeing the sites tomorrow. So the jury's still out on me having a future here." She paused. "What's really on your mind, Ellie? I can hear you chomping popcorn." Olivia donned her sunglasses to keep additional salespeople from gaining eye contact with her.

"I received an interesting e-mail from the editor of *Above & Beyond* magazine."

Olivia sat up and covered her other ear. "Isn't that the magazine you applied to with the Timbuktu article and photo proposal?"

"Yes. They're interested and want to have a phone interview with me tomorrow." Ellie chomped some more popcorn.

"Ellie, if they want an interview, they could offer you the project. Are you ready for that?" Olivia asked.

Ellie paused a beat. "I'm excited about the possibility—"

"But…"

"But I'm scared too. What if they pay my expenses, send me there, and I do the job but it's not good enough? And they'll assign an interpreter for me since I'm not great in French. What if we don't get along? Maybe I'm not ready."

"Ellie, your photography is superb. Your writing is in a dozen magazines. And you get along with everyone who crosses your path, even our grumpy old neighbor Mr. Oswald. You're exhausted, jet-lagged, and letting a case of nerves talk you out of an amazing opportunity. You need to quit eating popcorn, get some sleep, and start over in the morning. Ace the interview and book a ticket for Mali, West Africa.

This job can change your life. It's what you've dreamed about doing for years. Give it to the Lord and rest in Him. You're going to succeed."

"I needed to hear that, Liv. That's why I called. Thanks."

"No problem. The Lord has given you amazing talent. You can't hide it. Text me after your interview."

"You got it. I feel better. Love you. Bye."

Ellie's call ended. Olivia looked at her phone and smiled. Ellie always hung up fast.

The clear water looked so refreshing that she took her kikoi off and walked to the edge of the waves. Wading in about three feet, she stood, watching tropical fish swimming around her legs. Angelfish, clownfish, and yellow tang swam close, eating reef pods. It reminded her of her father's hundred-gallon saltwater tanks he had in his office when she was young. She'd gone to sleep many times on his couch, watching the fish while he worked at his desk. Then he'd carry her to bed while she pretended to be asleep but loved being held. Great memory.

She hurried to her chair; the beach waiter was bringing her a strawberry slush.

"This will refresh you, Ms. Stone."

"Perfect timing. Thank you, Julius." She reached into her bag and handed him a tip, then took a long drink, causing a brain freeze. *Ouch.* She finished it slower than she started, then took a nap under the swaying palm trees.

*****

Enjoying a samosa and some spice tea, Aga Kahn worked at his home office, planning an acquisition of another property in Stone Town. Some threatening could bring the price down; he'd have to visit the owner again. His cell vibrated in his pocket. "Yes."

"Aga Kahn, the Sahar is at the resort, in a lounge chair on the beach, asleep. She is not packing her luggage yet." Rahad paused. "You want me to keep watching her?"

"No. Complete my other directives. I plan to watch the docks later today."

"Yes, Aga Kahn. I will get it done." He ended the call.

Kahn checked his watch, stacked his papers, put them in his briefcase, and called for his driver. He had enough time to make a surprise visit to Stone Town before the ferry arrived.

*****

A warm shower after a day at the beach felt soothing. Olivia dressed for dinner and took a seat at her assigned table. The light breeze cooled her neck since her hair was up in a messy bun. Her large hoop earrings banged her skin, making her question her jewelry choice.

"Did you have a nice day, Ms. Stone?" The resort manager, Makau, bowed slightly as he greeted her.

"Yes, I did. I feel refreshed." She sat back for him to put her linen napkin across her lap, then laced her fingers on the tablecloth.

"You will enjoy Zanzibar." He opened a bottle of water and poured it for her. "Our soup is mushroom tonight. We also have roasted goat on the grill and fresh prawns as our specialty. Please enjoy."

She passed on the soup, skipped the salad, and went straight for the grilled vegetables and prawns but almost dropped her plate when she saw Aga Kahn staring at her direction. *He knows I didn't leave on the ferry today. He wants to frighten me into leaving tomorrow.* Goose bumps rose on her flesh as she strode to her table. Ignoring the Indian, she took her time trying to enjoy her meal. After having tea and dessert, she requested to see the manager.

"How can I be of service, Ms. Stone?" The manager waited.

"The Indian man has been watching me again tonight. Would you walk with me to my room, Bwana?" She put her cloth napkin on the table.

"Absolutely. Are you ready?"

She stood. "Yes, if you're free to be my escort."

"I'll lead the way." He turned toward her accommodations. "These lights were shining last night. I will have them checked immediately." The manager, Loy Makau, crunched glass under his shoes. He looked down. "I fear they have been broken with purpose."

When they neared her room, she gave him the key. He opened the door, turned on the light, and held the door for her to enter.

"No!" She stood, staring at a huge mess. "Someone has ransacked this room, Bwana. How did they get in?" The mattress was off the bed. Her suitcase had been emptied, and her clothes were strewn across the floor. Toiletries were scattered.

The manager checked the restroom as he called security. "Would you feel more secure if we moved you to another room? You cannot stay here."

"Yes, if you have a vacancy, and could we keep the location quiet?" Olivia's hands trembled.

"I'm sure we have a vacancy, and keeping the location silent is a good idea." He made another call to arrange alternate accommodations.

Olivia walked to the windows, being careful not to touch anything. "Bwana, two windows are unlocked. I made sure they were locked when I left the room. This frightens me."

"They were planning to return." He dialed another number and spoke as it rang through. "I'm calling the police. Please see if anything has been stolen."

She opened the safe. Her iPad and camera were still there. "Bwana, I think they tried to get into the safe. There are scratches by the lock."

Security arrived just before the police. They took pictures and brushed for fingerprints. Their antique methods would have been comical in different circumstances.

After waiting and watching for half an hour, Olivia approached the officer. "May I gather my clothes and toiletries?"

"Yes, but we would like to keep your suitcase until it is checked for prints." The police officer in charge spoke as he worked.

The manager gave her a laundry bag for her things. "I will collect the remainder of your belongings. Would you like to go to another room now?" He held up another key.

"That would be wonderful. I'm exhausted."

He led her to a different section of the resort and made sure she was inside, with the door locked, before he left her, returning to the scene of the crime.

Olivia checked the window locks, breathed a sigh of relief, and lay across the bed. Her phone chimed with a message.

This is Eli.
Are you okay?

She punched in his number.
"Hello. You okay?"

"No. I'm not okay. I had the manager walk me to my room. Some of the lights were out, making the hall pitch-black. When he opened my door, the room was ransacked. My clothes were all over the floor."

"No! Where are you now?"

"I'm in a new room. I think it's a presidential suite or something. It's plush, and extra locks have me confined. Hotel security and the police are working on the crime scene. I got my things out of the safe, my pajamas and toiletries off the floor, and left the rest until tomorrow. The manager told me he would secure my property."

"I'm sorry this happened. How are you now?"

"Still a bit shook. It angered me, until I found two windows unlocked. Then, I was scared. The manager said they were probably planning to return." She took a deep breath and blew it out.

"Is there anything I can do?" Eli asked.

"Pray that I can sleep tonight. I've got jet lag and a bad case of nerves."

"I'll do that. Do you feel safe now?"

"Yes. It's on the second floor, close to the lobby. They left me an air horn to use if I need assistance. I'm sure he's long gone, since the police are here." She sat up and removed her shoes.

"Olivia, what are your plans for tomorrow?"

"I was going to start touring the island, but I think I'll stay here and enjoy the beach or one of the pristine pools. This place is gorgeous."

"You're safe in crowds. Stay close to other people. Okay?"

"I can do that. The manager said he was hiring extra guards to secure the resort while I'm here."

"I'm glad." He paused. "Do you mind texting me when you wake up in the morning?"

"Sure. Thanks for checking on me."

"Sleep well, Olivia."

"Good night, Eli." She smiled, picturing the good-looking missionary, definitely a hero.

CHAPTER 3

"Fahad, did you find her passport?" Aga Kahn paced his bedroom.

"No. Unless it was locked in the safe, it wasn't in her room. She must be carrying it with her. I checked every possible place."

"You didn't break into the safe?"

"I was trying to when we heard someone coming and had to leave quickly. I left two windows unlocked, as you requested."

"I'm sure they've moved her to another room while they investigate. Your actions have frightened her. Now she knows she should have left on the ferry. Let's see if she leaves tomorrow. If she doesn't follow my directive, we'll make plans to eliminate this problem." Kahn sat on the side of his bed.

"You are a wise one, Aga Kahn."

"Tomorrow we will talk." Aga Kahn ended the call and turned out the light.

*****

Eli kept his phone with him until Olivia's text came through.

> Morning, Missionary Deckland.
> I slept well, and I'm ready for breakfast.
> The manager has hired extra guards.

No need to worry.
Isn't worrying a sin? Lol

Olivia

PS: Thanks again for helping me.

He smiled, put his hat on, and started moving the sticks and debris that were on the other side of the wall he was rebuilding around the church property. He needed help with the project, but the men in his church had jobs, and providing for their families took precedence. Piece by piece he cleared the land. When the last pieces had been removed, he stared at large tire tracks and indentions in the few cement blocks still standing. He grabbed his cell and took photos of his find along with exact measurements of the tracks.

Joy had suspected Aga Kahn ordered the destruction of the wall. He was desperate to force them to leave Zanzibar. Their success in converting Muslims to Christianity had fueled a fire in the angry man. Confronting him with the truth cost Joy her life. Proving it was going to be difficult.

Anger fueled Eli's labor under the scorching tropical sun. He put in seven long hours before calling it a day. After a much-needed shower, he added today's find to his computer, storing it in two places for safekeeping.

*****

A strong chlorine smell blew Olivia's direction as she chose a cushioned lounge chair and umbrella by the resort's beautiful pool. After applying a thick coat of sunscreen on her legs, she worked on her arms. Being close to the equator, where the sun's rays are ten times hotter than in America, she wanted to be protected.

"You need some help? I could do your back for you." A college-aged girl took the chair next to her. "Hi, I'm Scarlett."

"I'm Olivia, and that would be great. I use spray sunscreen on my back, but it's not as good as my lotion." Olivia handed the bottle to her. "I could help you too."

"That would be great. I'm going on the Safari Blue tour in about thirty minutes, and I need to be covered in sunscreen." Scarlett sat behind Olivia and applied the lotion to her back.

"What's the Safari Blue tour?"

"I've heard it's amazing. It costs seventy dollars to ride on a dhow, we'll swim with dolphins, have a seafood barbeque lunch on the beach, relax in a lagoon among the mangroves, then stop at a sandbar before we return to shore. Why don't you come with?" Scarlett gave the sunscreen to Olivia.

Olivia turned and applied sunscreen to Scarlett's back. "It sounds like fun. Are you sure there is room for one more?"

"Absolutely. We're taking a taxi."

She thought about it for a minute. "Okay, you talked me into it." Olivia smiled and closed the sunscreen. "I'll get some shillings out of my room safe and hurry back."

"Perfect."

She turned to leave, then pivoted. "You don't have any Dramamine, do you?"

"Yeah, in my backpack. I'll bring you some."

"Thanks."

Scarlett and her two girlfriends were waiting in the lobby. "Olivia, this is Lisa and Ava."

Olivia greeted the chatty trio as they boarded their taxi.

After a twenty-minute ride, they walked the gangplank onto the dhow, an open vessel with bench seats along the sides and around the base of the mainmast on the center-line. It seemed sturdy despite its weathered appearance. The staff of locals was friendly, though lacking a few teeth in their stained smiles. Snorkeling equipment and life jackets were distributed as they left the port.

"Olivia, what kind of camera is that?" Ava watched as Olivia put a disk into her camera.

She closed it. "It's a digital underwater camera that does videos and selfies." Olivia let her hold the camera. "If you ladies don't mind taking my picture from time to time, I'll film your memories and send them to you."

They chimed in, "Yeah," "Absolutely," "That would be great," "You bet."

Donning their masks and snorkels, they plunged into the water. Vibrant colors painted the afternoon. The turquoise water under a baby-blue sky set the stage as they swam with an array of gorgeous fish among colorful coral. When they added pink, blue, and yellow bathing suits to the scene, the photos were amazing.

The dolphins were fun as they interacted with the foursome. They pulled them through the water, jumped in sync, displaying their strength, and swam backward as the ladies laughed at them.

"I'm tired." Olivia climbed the rope ladder hanging from the side of the dhow. "But that was so much fun." She turned and helped her new friends on board. Their giggles and exhilaration bubbled between them. "I can check it off my bucket list!"

Scarlett hugged Olivia. "That was the best!"

After removing their equipment, they collapsed on the benches and leisurely enjoyed the ride until the aroma of grilled shrimp revived them.

"Lunch is ready. Allow us to help you disembark. The dhow moves with the waves. We will leave for the sandbar in one hour. Enjoy your lunch." The captain directed his passengers toward a pier.

Olivia stood and led the way. "It smells like fish and shrimp."

Scarlett's stomach growled. "My stomach thinks I forgot to eat."

The foursome was last to get off the vessel.

"Ladies, we've hung hammocks among the mangrove trees for you to relax until we depart for the sandbar." The captain motioned toward the area.

"Thank you. We'll enjoy the hammocks," Lisa told the captain.

Olivia chose a hammock close to the waves, where fiddler crabs and mudskippers played along the water's edge. Their pleasant afternoon was filled with lively conversations and laughter. Time on the sandbar darkened their tans as they strolled the snow-white sand, looking for shells. Weary from their day, Olivia bade her friends farewell as they reached the lobby of their resort.

"Thank you, Scarlett, for inviting me. I had a wonderful time. Give me your phone number at dinner and I'll send you the photos."

Lisa and Ava hugged her before going to their room.

Scarlett hesitated with Olivia. "I hope you don't mind me asking, but what are you doing in Zanzibar? We're on vacation, but I sense more purpose in your visit." Scarlet put her hand on Olivia's arm.

"I'm a flight attendant, but I'm considering making a job change and felt my answer was on this island. I want to make a difference somehow. So I'm using two weeks of leave to pursue whatever the Lord has for me." Olivia hoped her words made sense, because sometimes she doubted this pursuit herself.

"With your adventurous spirit and heart to leave a legacy, the Lord will guide you. I have no doubts. I'm glad our paths crossed." She hugged her again. "I'll see you at dinner." She went about three steps and pivoted. "God has a plan, Olivia, and He will see you through the ups and downs of your journey. You can trust Him." She turned and left.

As Scarlett disappeared down the hall, Olivia felt confirmed in her quest. As she strolled to her room, a song her grandmother used to sing came to mind. *I don't know about tomorrow, but I know who holds my hand.* She smiled.

*****

Judah ran Eli's direction when he stepped into the living room. Toy cars of all sizes were lined up, ready to be pushed across the coffee table at any moment.

"Cars, Dada, cars." Judah, dressed in a T-shirt and overalls, gave Eli three cars. He knew he'd been instructed to play with him.

"Mama?" Judah looked up at Eli.

"No, Judah. Mama is gone." Eli's heart hurt for his son. He made the appropriate car noises as they raced on the table, keeping his son's focus on his make-believe world, where cars put smiles on his sweet face.

Joy worried that Judah would scratch the table, but it didn't matter now. Eli planned to sell most of their belongings before they left for the States, and Judah's happiness was more important at this juncture.

His phone dinged with a message.

Hey, Eli,

I had a great day. Guards are everywhere.
I did the Safari Blue tour this afternoon.
It was fun.
I'm touring Spice Tour tomorrow. I'll be
with a group.

Olivia

Eli relaxed. He'd keep praying for the Lord to protect her.

Judah's favorite car rolled under the futon, and he stretched to retrieve it. Daddy came to the rescue again. Judah clapped his hands as if Eli had saved the world. His grin made everything worth it.

"Mama?" Judah looked at Eli.

Eli put Judah on his lap. "Your mama is in heaven. Olivia looks like your mama, but she's not her." He was running his car down Eli's arm. "I know you don't understand, but trust me, you are loved."

Judah turned and kissed Eli's cheek. "Love Dada."

Eli smiled. "Good talk, son."

Feeding him, watching him swim in the long African bathtub, and putting him to bed took most of the evening. Being both mom and dad took its toll on Eli. But making him feel secure was crucial.

When he stretched out across his bed, Eli's mind strayed to a pair of chocolate eyes, long brown hair with burgundy highlights, and a sweet smile. Olivia was different, very different from Joy. She was a shock and a pleasant surprise in one package. Her presence was confusing Judah. Maybe it was a good thing she didn't live here, he figured. She was confusing him too. He dozed off with his shoes still on.

*****

Aga Kahn stood in his regal robes, watching the crowd gathering at the port from his rooftop perch at an Indian restaurant. The American woman had yet to show. But it was early. He would savor his tea and enjoy the ocean breeze as he waited like a lion stalking his prey.

As the ferry approached the dock, the number of waiting passengers increased. But the Deckland woman wasn't among them. Aga Kahn watched the passengers disembark. When the captain allowed those departing to come aboard for the return trip, Aga Kahn checked each person meticulously.

Garbage burning sent smoke his direction, adding to his displeasure. As he kept his eyes on the scene before him, his rage built. *She did not obey. When will she learn I'm not a man to be ignored?*

His cell rang. "What!" Ali Kahn's temper laced his voice.

As he listened, he reached into a pocket in his robe for some shillings and slung thirty-five thousand Tanzanian shillings on the table. "She's on the Spice Tour? Do you see her?" Aga Kahn spoke, then listened. He looked at his watch. "Keep her in your sights. I'm coming in that direction, and I'll have a plan. Good work, Fahad." He hurried to his vehicle.

"Asim, take me to the Tangawizi Spice Farm near Dole Mosque in Stone Town, where people end the Spice Tour. And hurry."

Aga Kahn scrolled through the contact list on his cell and punched a number as they endured stop-and-go traffic.

"Hello, Officer Gichuhi. I need some assistance with a personal matter. Complete privacy is mandatory. Can I count on your help?" He listened and smiled. "I'll be downtown in a matter of minutes. Can you meet me in the waiting area for those on the Spice Tour near Dole Mosque in Stone Town? It is convenient since your office is near. I need you to apprehend an American woman and check her passport. Question her purpose for being in Zanzibar. It would secure a bonus for you if you understand my meaning." He paused. "See you there."

Talk yourself out of this fix, Mrs. Missionary.

*****

Dressed in capri pants, sandals, and a gauzy short-sleeved blouse, with her hair in her favorite messy bun, Olivia hurried to catch up with the tour guide. "Maria, you seem to love your job. You've made this tour informative and fun for the tourists. Great job. I had no idea this many spices came from Zanzibar. They don't taste as they smell."

"People are surprised by that. They think it will be the same. We choose our food mostly by smell." Her lightweight skirt flowed in the breeze.

"How long have you been working for Tangawizi Tours?" Olivia watched her expressions.

"Only two years, but I am hoping it will be my job for life. There are few jobs on the island. I am blessed to be chosen for this position." She looked to be in her midtwenties. Her uncovered head suggested her bent on Christianity. With lovely eyes and a winning smile, Olivia knew she would go far in life.

"So a job as a tour guide wouldn't be available for someone like me?"

Maria stopped walking and faced her. "Someone like you can get employment anywhere. Why would you want to take a job in Zanzibar and put me on the streets? That is what happens here. Unless you are starting a business that offers jobs to Zanzibaris, please don't consider this thought. I do not mean to sound harsh, but life is hard in third-world countries." She touched Olivia's arm before she continued the tour.

Olivia felt like she'd been sucker punched. Her technical research didn't give a complete cultural picture.

"Ladies, you will like this plant." Maria harvested a piece of fruit, opened it, and rubbed a metal bar the size of a Q-tip into the meat she harvested. "Now you apply this to your lips and it will stain them with a deep red color. It's free lipstick. Try it."

Olivia stepped forward and allowed Maria to paint her lips. "Thank you."

"I appreciate you for understanding my words. I meant no harm." She put the metal bar in her hand, making it a gift to Olivia, and smiled.

As they ended the tour, a thin barefoot Zanzibari man with ragged clothes climbed a tree, performing some acrobatic stunts, kicked his legs out, and hung from the treetops. He cut coconuts for everyone, opened them so they could drink the milk and eat the meat of the coconut.

Olivia felt the rough, hairy shell of the coconut. "This is amazing. I love it!" Olivia handed her phone to Maria. "Take a picture of me drinking coconut milk in front of this fuchsia bougainvillea."

"Thanks, Maria. I've enjoyed the tour, and I'll consider your concerns."

"You're welcome."

Maria turned and gave final greetings to the group and let them know that taxies and dolla dollas, small trucks with benches in the back for passengers, were ready to take them to their hotels.

When the tourists disbanded, Olivia selected a taxi and walked that direction. As she neared the cab, a police officer stepped in front of her, blocking her path.

"I need you to come with me. We need to check your passport, if you don't mind." His name tag said "Gichuhi"; his demeanor meant business.

"I do mind. Going with you is out of the question. My passport is current, and I purchased a visa before I arrived. Why would you need to detain me?" The police officer tried to grab her arm. She jerked back. Then she saw him. *Ali Baba.*

"My office isn't far. It's down the alley on the right. Let us get out of the blazing sun." He put his hand on his weapon and motioned for her to walk the cobblestone path in front of him. Aga Kahn led the way.

Perfect. With no hero insight, I'm following the man who wants me dead. Is this what it feels like to walk to a guillotine? This can't be good.

When Officer Gichuhi, Aga Kahn, and Olivia stepped into his stuffy office, the lack of air-conditioning caused her to perspire. Or was it the closeness to Aga Kahn?

The officer took a seat in his chair behind his brown desk. The walls and concrete floors were also painted brown. Two chairs offered extra seating. Olivia chose to stand. They were covered in cracked brown vinyl that would probably tear her clothes and pinch her skin.

"May I see your passport and visa?" Officer Gichuhi held his hand out, waiting for her to put them in his palm.

Olivia pulled her documents from her bag and gave them to the officer, pushing the Record button on her phone as the men focused on her photo inside the passport.

"The visa is in the back. Has Aga Kahn requested for me to be detained? I told him I'm not who he thinks I am. He's just upset because he got rid of Joy Deckland and I showed up looking like her. If he weren't guilty, would he be so worried?" She waited, hoping he would reveal the truth that would give Eli the closure he needed by getting a confession.

She faced Aga Kahn. "Did you find what you were looking for when your men searched my hotel room? Or are you angry because I didn't leave on the ferry as you demanded?" She stared him down. "Are you going to bruise my arm again like you did when you threatened me on the road at the port? A police officer is watching."

Officer Gichuhi stopped scanning her passport and stared at Olivia, then at Aga Kahn. It was obvious he didn't know what Kahn had been doing.

Kahn slapped his hand on the officer's desk. "I warned you to leave. You are living dangerously by staying on my island." He moved closer to Olivia.

Officer Gichuhi stood. "May I remind you, Kahn, this is a police station. It's not a place to make veiled threats." He waited for Kahn to back off, then resumed his task.

"Gichuhi, I have to protect our heritage, our way of life. She must understand my position." He stood silent, but his clenched fists betrayed his anger.

Olivia fanned herself with a folder she took off the officer's desk. She tapped her foot as moments slipped by like the perspiration making its way down her back. Growing impatient, she turned to the police officer. "Are my documents in order, Bwana? I have plans for the evening." She extended her hand, waiting for him to return her passport.

He stood. "Yes, Olivia Stone, your documents are up-to-date. The name Olivia Stone reminds me of Livingstone. Are you related to the missionary David Livingstone?" He put her passport in her hand.

She put her passport away as she answered the officer. "Not that I know of. But I would be proud to be related to him. May I go?"

Aga Kahn interrupted. "Is that your connection with Deckland? The church where he works is on the David Livingstone property. Livingstone laid a foundation for Christianity in Zanzibar. The government gave the acre as a burial place for Christians."

"I don't know anything about Deckland's church. I met him for the first time when I got off the ferry." She turned to leave. Pivoting, she turned back. "Officer Gichuhi, would you tell your Indian friend who I am so he will leave me alone and let me enjoy my vacation, or do I need to press charges?"

"Pressing charges will not be necessary, Ms. Stone." Gichuhi stood. "You are free to go." He motioned toward the door.

Aga Kahn stepped in front of the door.

Olivia glared at him. "Move!" She stood firm, not knowing the source of her sudden courage. His dark eyes held pure evil, and evil feasted on fear. Without breaking their gaze, she lifted an arched brow and moved closer.

First, to break off the stare-down, he stepped aside.

She left the office on the uneven sidewalk and waved for a taxi, still in shock that she'd stared down a killer. *What's wrong with me?* Her knees were weak and her hands trembled as she closed the taxi door. Risking a look, she turned and met Aga Kahn's piercing gaze.

"Where I take you?" The driver's broken English made her wonder if he could find her destination.

Olivia paused and let out a shaky breath she didn't realize she was holding, then pulled out her phone and pulled up Eli's address, which he'd given her. She read off the address, and he took off, stirring dust in his wake. Olivia turned to see Ali Baba wiping his face. She smiled.

Was she making a mistake showing up at Eli's house unannounced? He needed to know what happened. Right? Maybe it would be okay. She wouldn't stay long, unless he swept her off her feet and declared his undying love. Undying—his wife just died. *What am I thinking?*

"Bwana, maybe I should go back to my hotel."

He'd honked the horn and was pulling the cab into Eli's compound.

Too late.

*****

"No, this can't be right." Aga Kahn dropped the copy of the passport on the desk. "Gichuhi, I thought I had the proof I needed. Can I have a copy of this?"

"Absolutely." He turned to the copier, pressed a button, then handed him a copy.

"Could she have gone to the States, changed her name, and gotten a new passport? It's been over a year." Aga Kahn paced the small sweltering office. He shot a glance at the open window and swiped moisture from the back of his neck. "It has to be her." He'd felt an eerie feeling when he locked eyes with her. Enough playing games. This time she would stay dead.

The police officer tapped a pencil against his desk so hard the lead broke. "It is possible. Would you like me to do some research on Olivia Stone? It will take about twenty-four hours for a basic search."

"Yes, do that, and keep it between us." He put some Tanzanian bills into Gichuhi's hand. "Can you run comparative research on Joy Deckland at the same time? Look for anything suspicious. I'm sure it is the same person. Call me as soon as you know anything."

"Yes, Aga Kahn. I'll do it right away."

Aga Kahn lowered his voice. "I let go your reprimand earlier since Ms. Stone was here. But do I need to remind you who I am and what I can do?"

"No need for that, Aga Kahn." He pushed the On button on his desktop computer to begin his search.

Aga Kahn left without further conversation and slid into his luxury sedan. "Amis, home for the evening."

"Ndio, Bwana. Yes, sir."

Kahn pressed a number into his phone. "Fahad, did you get a copy of Joy Deckland's passport picture?" He listened. "Great. Bring it by tomorrow. I'm retiring early." He hung up without a goodbye.

*****

"Olivia, you okay?" Eli stood on the porch, in sweatpants, a T-shirt, and flip-flops.

"Yes. I need to talk to you." She paid the driver and walked toward Eli. "I was escorted to the police station when the Spice Tour ended by Officer Gichuhi and Aga Kahn. I recorded the conversation."

The ocean breeze blew hair into her face that had escaped the messy bun. She put the strand behind her ear. Her capri pants, sandals, and the flowy blouse weren't what she would have worn if she knew she'd be stopping at Eli's home.

Eli opened the screen door and held it for her. "Let's go inside. Aga Kahn's men have been coming by frequently. I wouldn't want our conversation overheard."

She walked up the steps to the porch. "I'm sorry for barging in without calling."

"I'm glad you did. I've been concerned about your safety. I uncovered some evidence today myself." He led her through the living room with terrazzo floors, concrete walls, bars on the windows, and a bulb hung from the ceiling. "Judah's still napping," he whispered and led her to a bedroom. "My office is in my bedroom. Please don't feel uncomfortable. We're not alone. Frances is in the kitchen."

"It's fine, Eli. I want you to hear the conversation I recorded." She followed him into the bedroom-slash-office.

"Excuse my stacks of boxes. Frances has been packing Joy's things for my move to the States." Eli stepped to an armoire and opened the doors. On the inside of the doors and the back of the large piece of furniture was an evidence board like detectives create on television crime shows.

"Wow. You're serious about this, aren't you?" She stepped toward the armoire to read the evidence he had gathered.

"Yes, very." He pointed to the board. "This is the time-line I created before and after Joy's murder. This list is of peculiar things that have occurred, which include the destruction of the security wall around the church grounds and a fire at the church. I rebuilt the church first, which took almost a year. Now I'm rebuilding the wall." He pointed to another section. "I started a new timeline when you arrived."

"You think it's connected, don't you?" She waited.

"I do." He massaged the back of his neck. "I uncovered some more clues today, literally." He tapped the keyboard of his laptop, and the screen came alive.

Olivia leaned toward the screen, breathing in the masculine scent of Eli's soap. "What are we looking at?"

"Today when I cleared the area outside the fence I've been repairing, I found wide tire tracks and indentions in the part of the wall that's still standing. I took these pictures and measured the tracks. I thought Aga Kahn had ordered the crashing of our security wall. Joy said Kahn would go to extreme measures to make us leave Zanzibar."

Olivia covered her mouth. Then put her hand on his arm. "And he killed her. I'm sorry, Eli. This has to be difficult for you, to lose the love of your life and not be able to prove who did it."

"I appreciate your concern. I do want justice for Joy. But…" He paused.

She waited. "Eli?"

He looked at Olivia. "Joy and I grew up together, graduated in the same class, and attended the same university. She was my best friend. We made a pact that when we reached thirty years of age, if neither of us was married, we'd get married and save the world, side by side. Joy was not the love of my life." He held her gaze. "But I appreciate your concern." Eli cleared his throat and changed the subject. "I need to hear what you recorded."

She pulled out her phone and played the recording.

"He didn't deny his treatment of you and probably still thinks you're Joy. Bringing his wrongdoings to light in front of a police officer infuriated him. I hate to say this, but standing up to him probably made things worse. But that officer will report what you accused him of to his superior, which is good. Your looks have put a target on your back. So be careful."

"I think I'll change hotels tomorrow. Aga Kahn could have an inside man working at Ocean Paradise who helped his men get into my room." She pocketed her phone.

"That's a good idea." He turned his laptop off. "I hear a little boy. He'd love to see you again. Are you okay with that? He's been sleeping so peacefully since he saw you at the port."

"He's precious. I'd love to, if you're sure. I don't want him to be upset when I leave."

"Well, you have to pass through the living room to exit, so let's go play with some matchbox cars. Shall we?" Eli stood and led the way.

*****

Judah was eating a snack at the table when Olivia and Eli found him. He was singing and playing with a car on the table beside his plate. Eli took a seat beside him.

"Hi, Dada." He hugged Eli. "Car go fast. See?" He sent it flying across the table, then clapped his hands.

"It's a fast car." Eli put his hand on Judah's shoulder. "Judah, our friend Olivia is here."

Judah looked at his dad, as if it didn't register with him.

Eli motioned for Olivia to join them. She eased into the room and took a seat on the other side. "Hello, Judah."

He looked at her, smiled, and launched himself into her arms.

"Mama, Mama."

Olivia held him, looking at Eli over his head.

Judah turned and sat on her lap, pulled his plate close, and finished his snack, mumbling words and making car sounds as he played.

"He is such a sweet child, Eli. You've done a great job with him."

"Thank you. He was almost five months old when we lost Joy. He carries her picture with him." Eli looked around and saw the photo, picked it up, and showed it to Olivia.

Her eyes grew wide. "I do look like her."

"Like a twin." He took the picture, looked at it, then compared it to Olivia. "It's uncanny."

"This isn't my natural hair color, if that helps."

"Nope. It doesn't help. Joy put burgundy highlights in her hair too."

Judah slipped out of her lap but pulled her hand so she would follow. He patted the futon for her to sit. She obeyed. He brought her several cars so they could play. And they did for an hour.

Olivia laughed at his antics and enjoyed the time.

When Eli joined them, Judah took him two cars.

"His mother may be gone, but he is a happy boy, pure innocence."

"He is a gift from the Lord." Eli lined Judah's cars up for him, then looked at Olivia. "What about you, Olivia Stone? You have a husband or a child waiting for you to return?"

"No. I haven't been as fortunate as you. Flying the African skies doesn't allow much time to date, so finding that special someone hasn't happened for me yet." She handed Judah a car he'd dropped. "As for children, they're not in the cards for me."

"You would need to be home every day. Flying does limit you. I've never thought about it."

Frances chose that moment to announce dinner was ready.

"Oh, sorry. I've overstayed my welcome. I'll call a cab and get back to my hotel." She stood and pulled out her cell phone.

Judah grabbed two handfuls of cars and went to stand by Olivia.

"Please join us for dinner. It won't be fancy, but there's always plenty." Eli picked up Judah and waited with two pair of amber eyes begging.

"Are you sure? I don't want to impose." Olivia moved toward the door, poised to leave.

"Look at this little face. Can you tell him no?" Eli put his head next to Judah's.

Olivia smiled. "You don't fight fair, Mr. Missionary."

He shrugged and smiled.

Does he have any idea how tempting it would be to love both of these Decklands? Those broad shoulders, his winning smile, and that strand of hair falling on his forehead put him in the eye-candy category. He's quite the man of integrity to boot. Guard your heart, Olivia. You leave Zanzibar in nine days since the tour-guide possibilities are looking bleak.

Frances served baked fish with lemon, seasoned vegetables, and creamy macaroni with thick tortilla bread, called chapatis. Judah was quite the eater, although he made a serious mess of his clothes and the floor.

Eli seemed to know exactly what Judah wanted and served him with ease. When the boy tapped the ends of his fingers together, Eli gave him more.

Eli noticed Olivia watching them. "Joy taught him sign language. It makes mealtime quieter. He asks for more, says please and thank you, and signs 'All done.' Watch for it."

When his macaroni was gone, Judah shook his hands.

"All done?" Olivia said.

"Yep, he's done. Now he's saying thank you." Eli started cleaning his hands and face. When he took him out of his high chair, Judah held out his hand. Eli put his matchbox cars in it, and he took off for the living room, his playground.

"So cute. You're blessed, Eli."

He looked at Olivia. "The Lord's blessings overflow sometimes." He winked at her and joined Judah in the living room. Judah was playing cars while Eli was playing his cards—with a small measure of success.

CHAPTER 4

Olivia helped Frances clear the table. "I loved the vegetables, Frances. What seasoning did you use?"

Frances wiped her hands on her apron, opened a cabinet, took out a small jar, and turned to Olivia. "Mama, I use white pepper and a pinch of this Asian seasoning. Not too much makes it good."

"Thanks, Frances." She brought in the last of the fish and macaroni. The simple kitchen was plain, but clean and efficient. Olivia made three trips, bringing in the last of the dishes.

"Put those on the counter by the sink and I'll put it away. You need to spend more time with Bwana and our sweet boy."

Olivia smiled and put her hand on Frances's arm. "You love them, don't you?"

"I do. They are special to my heart. Go make them smile again." Frances put a bowl of ice cream and a spoon in Olivia's hand, dismissing her from kitchen duty. "Judah's favorite."

Olivia stood at the door of the living room, watching Eli play with Judah. Their bond was evident, their laughter real. Judah spotted Olivia first. "Mama!" Judah ran to her.

"Frances sent you some ice cream." Olivia waved the spoon at Judah, sat on the sofa, and began feeding Judah small bites after Eli put him on the end of the coffee table across from her. "You're like a baby bird, always ready for another bite." He wiggled with excitement, and Olivia missed his mouth. Ice cream ran down his chin and dripped onto his shirt. "I think we're making a mess, little boy." She caught a drop of the creamy dessert and licked her finger. "It's good, but not very sweet."

"American ice cream may be too sweet for him." Eli reached for a basket and put some toy cars in it while Olivia fed Judah.

"Try sherbet first. Then maybe some sugar-free ice cream." She scraped the last of the ice cream into the spoon.

Judah tapped the end of his fingers together, asking for more.

"Okay, open wide." She fed him the last few bites while Eli retrieved a wet rag.

He wiped his hands and face, but it was also on his hair. "I think it's hopeless." He pulled Judah's clothes off, all except his cloth diaper. "Frances, will you put Judah in a bubble bath? I'll be there in a few minutes to relieve you." Eli put Judah in her arms. He protested, but Eli changed his focus. "Bubble bath?"

The sweet boy clapped his hands. "Bubba, bubba." He told Frances. "Bubba." She took him down the hall, with him jabbering all the way.

"It's getting late. I need to get back to the resort." Olivia called a taxi while Eli gathered more of Judah's cars. She picked up a couple of cars and put them in Eli's hand. The connection sizzled between them.

Eli stared into her eyes. "Olivia, I..."

"Eli, I may look like Joy, but I'm not her. I can't fill her shoes." She picked up her purse and started for the door.

He grabbed her hand, stopping her escape. "I'm not asking you to be her. You're your own person. Yes, you resemble her, your looks have made you a target, and I feel responsible for that. But I don't see Joy when I look at you. I don't hear her when you speak. Please trust me on this."

She hesitated. "Are you sure?" She put her hand on his and held his gaze.

"I'm sure."

"Okay. It does give me comfort to know you've got my back with Ali Baba."

He smiled. "Call him what you want to, but don't underestimate his power or his reach." Eli walked her to the front porch to await her taxi. "What's your plan for tomorrow?"

"I'm going to move to Dream of Zanzibar Resort after breakfast."

"That's an amazing resort, much more secure, but pricey." He raised his eyebrows.

"It's my vacation. I'm not worried about the cost. Dream of Zanzibar is gated and seems more secure."

"You'll be in the lap of luxury. And yes, security's tight. Good idea."

"I'm touring Stone Town after lunch and doing some shopping. I'll be with a group, and I will ride the hotel shuttle." Olivia moved closer to the porch steps.

"Watch your back. Proof of your identity may not get Kahn off your trail." He massaged the back of his neck.

"You massage your neck when you're concerned. I'll be careful. You do the same. You need to get Judah off this island."

"You're right. I'm finishing the security wall, taking care of some personal business matters, and packing. My replacement will arrive in about a month. I'd hoped to be able to have enough proof to convict Joy's murderer before I left. I'm not sure I can do that without risking Judah's safety."

"Some things you have to give to God and let Him handle it. Don't you preach that at your church?" She smiled.

"Every week."

A horn honked at the gate. The night guard hurried to open it.

"Thank you for dinner. It was wonderful. Judah's adorable. I enjoyed the evening with both of you." She squeezed his hand before taking the steps off the porch.

"You're welcome." He paused. "Olivia?"

She pivoted. "Yes."

"You want to go to Freedom Island on Saturday? I'm not working and could use a break. We could have dinner if you like. You need to see more of the sights before you leave."

Olivia paused, smiled at him. "Sounds great. Be at my hotel around nine, right after breakfast. And we'll enjoy the day." She opened the door to the cab and turned back toward Eli. "Where are you going when you leave here, Eli?"

He smiled. "I know what you're thinking. How can I leave this mansion?" He extended his arm toward the tin roof and peeling paint.

She laughed.

"Seriously, I'll go back to Texas, then regroup. No definite plans yet. Praying about that." He stepped off the porch. "What about you?"

"I think I'm in the same boat."

"Well, I think I'm going to keep my distance." He stepped back. "You get seasick on boats."

Olivia laughed and closed the taxi door.

*****

Eli finished Judah's bath and got him into bed.

"Mama?" Judah asked.

Eli sighed. "Ms. Olivia had to leave. Didn't you have fun tonight?"

Judah clapped his chubby hands and grabbed his favorite blanket.

"Car?"

Eli put a car in each of his hands, brushed his strawberry-blond hair off his forehead, and kissed him—a nightly ritual. After saying a prayer over him, he eased out of his room.

The house seemed empty since Olivia left. She fit in perfectly. *Lord, I'm trusting You with the future, mine, Judah's, and Becca's.*

He opened his laptop and enlarged the evidence he'd found earlier by the wall. Calculating the measurements and looking up SUV models on the island, he narrowed down the trucks that could make the indentions on the wall and would also have tire tread the width of the tracks he'd uncovered. "There's a nick in the right front tire." He smiled. "Find that tire, find the guilty party." He talked to himself.

Aga Kahn keeps his vehicles under lock and key. He'd have to see the truck in town, which might prove challenging. But one photo could tip the scales his direction. Maybe a drive through town was warranted.

He powered down the laptop and went to the kitchen for some of that ice cream. It didn't compare to ice cream in America, but Judah enjoyed it. Or maybe it was Olivia feeding it to him that made it special. He knew it would for him. Maybe he needed to step up his game. But who would want a single father with no direction for his future?

*****

She got what she paid for. Olivia loved the Dream of Zanzibar Resort. The grounds were covered with lush grass, perfectly manicured, with wild date palms and coconut palms. Seeing blue waves with white foam splashing the coast drew her like a magnet to the soft powder, cooled by the dancing branches of the palms. Thatched umbrellas for sunbathers dotted the beach, adding an African touch to the vast mixture of culture as yachts cruised off-shore and tourists skimmed the water on Jet Skis.

Her suite had a jacuzzi for her to use as she enjoyed the seascape outside her windows. Complete with Wi-Fi and large television, with American movies for evenings and rainy days. The elegance of candlelight, flowers, a fruit tray, and chilled juice created a dreamy ambiance.

Olivia relaxed oceanside under swaying palms, enjoying a cold soft drink while watching the waves. Two Zanzibari men handfishing in their dugout canoe brought in three good-size fish while riding the waves. Sand crabs and seagulls played hide-and-seek, the gulls trying to catch the crabs and them ducking into holes in the sand to escape being captured. The salty breeze under an azure sky created a postcard-perfect setting. It was luxurious. Peaceful.

Hearing voices and silverware clanging against dishes, she went to have lunch poolside.

"Table for one?" The host waited for her response.

"Yes, I'm alone."

He picked up a menu and some wrapped silverware. "Follow me, please." He led her to the best seat in the outdoor restaurant with a turquoise umbrella and held her chair for her. "I hope you enjoy your meal."

"Thank you. This is beautiful."

As she dined, no matter if it was breakfast, lunch, or dinner, she realized presentation and quality of the cuisine would challenge the best America offers. It was an ambiance that needed to be shared by couples in love and authors of romantic fiction.

Her mind went to Eli, an amazing man of integrity. Couple that with his beautiful eyes, masculine scent, and alluring smile, then add Judah to the mix with his bubbly personality, making them a dynamic duo invading her lonely heart. The total package. She sighed and perused the menu. *If only.*

"Welcome, Ms. Stone. Please take a seat in the front." The resort manager ushered the tour group into the van. "I hope you enjoy your afternoon." He closed the van door and waved as they departed.

The Stone Town Tour shuttle was filled with a German couple who couldn't speak English, three college students studying Islam, a pair of honeymooners, and Olivia. She met the guide, a Zanzibari woman about thirty years of age.

After introducing herself as Happy, she gave instructions about the afternoon. "We will tour casually, stopping to shop from kiosks and vendors along the way. I will give you interesting facts concerning our history, customs, and foods as we tour. Feel free to ask questions."

Happy was dressed like an American millennial with her holey jeans, bangle bracelets, and great makeup.

Olivia walked close so she could hear her commentary, hoping to strike up a conversation. About thirty minutes into the tour, they stopped at a leather shop for the men in the group to make purchases.

"Hello, Happy. I'm Olivia. Your smile is contagious, like a ray of sunshine in a dark place."

Happy smiled. "I have many reasons to smile. I have a job, I have friends, and I have Jesus."

"I do too. I've only encountered a few Christians in Zanzibar. It's great to meet you." Olivia hugged her. "So are tour guide jobs hard to get on the island?"

"Yes, very hard. Once you get employment in Zanzibar, you work very hard to keep the job for many years. Another job may not be found."

"You're so good at this assignment. I'm sure you will last," Olivia said.

Happy thanked her and took them to the next stop, sharing the love of the Lord among the group when given the opportunity. Olivia smiled, her decision made. She wouldn't take her job for anything. It was time to rethink her idea of getting employment in Zanzibar.

Happy talked about the Anglican Cathedral of Christ Church, which was built on the location of the whipping post of the slave market, one of the most famous slave monuments in the world. A cemetery and a smaller church sat on land connected to the historic sanctuary.

"Happy, what church is this in the shadow of the cathedral?" Olivia stepped closer to the guide.

Happy smiled. "This is my church. The Christian church. I was deaf when I was born. My grandmother took me to their first meetings, and Jesus healed me. I have served the Lord since that day."

"That's incredible. I'm so glad for you. I was in a car accident when I'd just turned two years old and got a head injury that caused me to go blind. The doctors called it Terson syndrome. A surgical procedure gave me sight when I was nine. The blindness made me appreciate the beauty of God's creation all the more. I see things others miss because they take details for granted." Olivia ran her hand over the cold blocks of the security wall. Hearing someone banging, she let her eyes go to a sweating American man putting a cement block into the far wall. *Eli.*

As if sensing her watching him, he turned and waved.

Olivia smiled and waved.

"You know my pastor, the missionary?" Happy asked.

"Yes. I met them when I arrived at the port. Judah calls me Mama when he sees me." Olivia smiled. "He's so cute."

"I can see why. You look like Mama Joy."

"It's so sad about his wife." Olivia turned and followed Happy to the front of the tour group.

"Her death changed him. His grief was almost palpable. But he keeps going."

"Happy, where can I hire some men to help him rebuild the security wall?" Olivia kept pace with her.

"What a great gesture. I will help you with that after the tour. That is kind of you." Happy turned and talked to her group. "Next, we will take some time at a souvenir shop. All things crafted in Zanzibar can be purchased here. So much history and the social status of the occupants living in Stone Town are prevalent in the architecture, especially on their ornate doors."

At the Memories of Zanzibar souvenir shop, Olivia bought a small replica of a door to remember the tour. She purchased a scarf to wear on her coat when cold weather chilled the air, and another kikoi to wear over her bathing suit, similar to the ones she bought on the beach.

"Stone Town is an amazing place where Arabic, African, Indian, and European cultures live comfortably together," Happy told the group.

Enjoying the day, Olivia almost forgot the threat Aga Kahn and his men had presented. *Almost.*

*****

Three Zanzibaris, with work gloves in hand, approached Eli as he took a water break and rested in the shade of a Baobab tree.

"Habari, Bwana. Hello. My name is Isaac. This is Omar and Samuel. Their English is not understandable, but they are good workers, and their children are hungry. We have been hired to help you in this work." Isaac eyed Eli, an American who was doing the work of a common laborer.

"Who hired you?" Eli waited.

"Our friend Happy sent us. She has shillings to give us when the job is done." Isaac grinned, two teeth missing causing his smile to look like a picket fence.

Eli offered the men a bottle of water, then gave instructions. Isaac interpreted for him. With them working side by side, the wall was completed within five hours of work by the four men. It would have taken Eli another week to do the job alone.

"Thank you, men, for your hard work today. You have been a blessing to me and this church. I hope you will join us for service this Sunday." Eli shook their hands as Isaac interpreted his words. "We have Swahili and English speakers and great music."

Eli planned to recognize them if they attended. He had a suspicion who funded the repairs. He smiled and headed home, in need of a shower, but relieved the security of the church grounds was complete. *Thanks, Olivia.*

*****

Excited about the day with Eli, Olivia was up early, dressed, and had her handbag packed. She hurried to the poolside restaurant for breakfast and watched lovebirds in the trees while her fried eggs were being prepared. Their juice was

76

fresh squeezed, and the locally grown coffee tasted like pure perfection. With a few minutes to spare, she returned to her room for some sunblock so she could reapply it later as needed. She looked down to find her key, looked up, and came face-to-face with Aga Kahn.

"You!" Olivia's breath caught. "Leave me alone!"

He grabbed Olivia by the throat and pressed her back against the wall.

She struggled to breathe, kicking his shins, her flip-flops doing little damage.

"The photos are the same. You changed your name. Get off my island or else—"

Eli rammed into the Indian, slamming him to the sidewalk. "Or else what, Aga Kahn? Will she meet the same fate that ended Joy's life?"

Olivia bent at the waist, sucking in air.

Aga Kahn was scrambling to stand.

"I'm reporting this attack, Kahn. Security will be increased. You've gone too far this time. She will press charges."

Aga Kahn stood. "It's time to leave Zanzibar, Deckland. And take her with you." He stomped away forcefully, dusting dirt from his robes.

Eli took Olivia's key and helped her into the room. "Lie on your bed against the pillows. I'll get you some water."

Olivia was shaking as she reclined on the pillows. Eli brought the water and sat on the edge of her bed as she took a drink.

"I was petrified. I couldn't breathe, Eli. I didn't know if he was trying to choke me or break my neck." Tears rolled down her cheeks. "What if you hadn't shown up?"

He wiped the moisture from her face. "You're safe now. Relax and try to breathe normally." He took the water bottle and opened the window, then returned to his seat on her bed.

"Thanks. The breeze helps. Is my throat red?"

He leaned in and examined both sides. "Yes. The imprint of his hands is turning red. It may be an ugly bruise." He sat up straight again.

"Take pictures of both sides. Document the time the attack occurred. You can add this to your collection of evidence. If it bruises, you need to photograph it again."

He reached for his phone. "Good idea." He moved her hair aside and took several shots, then moved to the opposite side before taking an additional photo of her face.

She smiled. "That's not my neck, Eli."

He winked. "I might need it as evidence."

"Of what?"

"That a pretty woman with a kind heart invaded my world and helped me find my smile again." He checked his phone screen. "Yep, perfect picture."

Olivia pulled her phone out of her bag. "Okay, smile, Mr. Missionary." She took a couple of photos and checked the screen. She showed him the one where he winked at her. "Do missionaries flirt?"

"I was a man before I became a missionary, so yes, they do." He laughed.

He took another picture of Olivia. "I love your smile, and my plan worked."

"What worked?" She put her phone in her bag.

"I distracted you, and you've stopped trembling."

Olivia raised her hands and saw they had stopped shaking. She smiled at Eli. "You're awful sneaky for a man of the cloth."

"It was in my job description."

She laughed. "Why did you come to my room this morning?"

"When I pulled into the parking lot, I saw one of Aga Kahn's men waiting by an SUV I've been watching for. It may be the truck that crashed into the security wall around my church. Since you weren't at breakfast, I asked for your room number and ran."

"You saved my life. How can I thank you?"

"I think you already did. You funded the workers that helped me finish the security wall at my church. So now I owe you." He took her hand and squeezed it.

"It wasn't much. I'm glad it helped."

"It did. It gives me peace of mind knowing the grounds are secure again." He leaned forward and kissed her forehead. "Well, Olivia Stone, are you ready for a great day?"

"You still want to go?"

"Absolutely." He stood, took her hands, and pulled her up to a standing position, holding her hands in case she was still shaky. His actions put them face-to-face.

She wanted to memorize the moment as she looked up at his handsome features. "I'm glad I can breathe now."

"Why is that?"

"You smell really good, Deckland."

"Thanks. I try to shower at least once every two weeks, whether I need it or not." He smiled. "And for the record, you don't smell so bad yourself."

"Thank you."

He released one of her hands and put a strand of her hair behind her ear.

She warmed at his touch. "You can rescue me anytime."

"I think we'd better get moving." He spoke but didn't move.

"Good idea." Olivia waited.

He stepped back, ending the moment.

*****

Aga Kahn slid into the SUV. "Take me home, Amis." He fastened his seat belt and made a phone call. "She still lives. Deckland interrupted me, and I couldn't finish the job. Have you heard from Officer Gichuhi?" He waited. "Call him back and tell him to notify you when he has the information. Then, retrieve it and bring it to my home. I will be waiting." He slapped the flip phone closed.

He watched the scenes of Zanzibar pass his window. The people of the island moved about the marketplaces, buying and selling, friendly banter filling the air. *Do they understand all that I do for them? Probably not. My success preserves the legacy of our forefathers. I must succeed.*

As they neared his home, his cell phone's ring brought him back to business. "Yes."

"Aga Kahn, I did as you requested. The report was delivered. I'll be at your home in a few minutes."

"That makes me glad. Thank you, Fahad. I await your arrival."

When they reached his home, a two-story white-stucco structure with expensive adornments, Asim opened his door, moved aside, and bowed until he passed. The house help took over from there, dusting his robes and sandals. "Prepare masala tea for two people. I am having a guest."

Fahad entered the conference room, bowed, and brought Aga Kahn the envelope Officer Gichuhi had prepared for him.

"Thank you, Fahad. Have some tea while I study these documents." Kahn read the pages twice, then compared the two photos, Joy Deckland's and Olivia Stone's, under a bright light. "I was correct in my first assessment. Their noses are a bit different, the eye color isn't the same, and they have different names. Those things could be easily altered in the States, and anyone can change their name. Both women are from Texas. I keep going back to the boy's reaction. A child knows his own mother. It's her. I'm sure of it." He folded the documents.

Fahad received a text. "May I take this?"

"Yes, since I'm still drinking my tea."

Fahad typed a return message. "The message was from Zubair. Olivia has left Dream of Zanzibar Resort with Eli Deckland. He did not hear where they were going."

Aga Kahn slammed his cup into the saucer, breaking the cup. Fahad called for the worker and gathered the broken china. He put the pieces on the worker's tray and got Aga Kahn another cup of his favorite brew.

"Zanzibar doesn't need Deckland and his message. His departure will mark a great day for Islam on my island."

*****

During the half-hour boat ride to Prison Island, Olivia enjoyed the wind blowing through her hair, giving a reprieve from the tropical heat. Or maybe the warmth was coming from the hunk who was standing right behind her, giving commentary about their excursion.

"Prison Island is called Changuu. It was where rebellious prisoners were kept until they could be shipped abroad or sold as slaves. Later, they housed the terminally ill in these buildings, those suffering from contagious diseases and yellow fever. Today, it's a vacation spot, with tourists using the quarantine houses as guesthouses. It's also the home of the Aldabra giant tortoises given to Zanzibar from the governor of Seychelles." He wiped drops of water off Olivia's arm from waves that sent spray their direction.

"You're full of information today. Did you and Joy come to Prison Island often?"

"Only once. Life was busy with our mission assignment." He got quiet.

Olivia turned to look at his face. "You miss her, don't you?" She held his gaze.

"Joy was my best friend. I miss doing missions with her. We were a great working team, understood each other." He looked toward their destination.

"I'm sorry, Eli."

"Thanks."

The boat eased toward a pier. It hit the pilings a couple of times before the captain and his men had it securely tied off. Eli stepped out first, turned, took Olivia's hand, and assisted her as she left the rocking boat and stepped onto the pier.

Olivia eyed some benches on the sand. "Could we sit for a few minutes?"

"You seasick?"

"Just a bit."

He didn't let her hand go, and she didn't protest, as they maneuvered through the tourists off-loading the old boat. Eli brushed the bench with a palm leaf that had fallen.

Olivia took in the scene. "I love swaying palm trees in Africa. They're taller than in the States or at the resorts in Mexico. You can see a clear sky with no smog, where clouds ease across the horizon, with seagulls and egrets enjoying the view."

"Only the African skies have this view. People can tell you about it, but you have to travel to the continent to see the difference." Eli rubbed his thumb over the back of her hand as they talked, sending warm sensations up her arm.

She hoped he wasn't reliving his time in this tourist site with Joy. She stood, breaking from his firm grip. "I feel better. Ready to get started?"

"Absolutely. How about we tour the prison-slash-hospital first? I'd like to get your picture behind bars." He smiled as they walked toward the buildings. "Then you can feed the tortoises before we have lunch at the Rock, a former fisherman's post. There are only twelve tables, so I made a reservation. Their food is great."

"Sounds like a plan."

Inside the ancient structure, they joined a group with a guide, who filled in the blanks in Eli's commentary about the prison, slave trade, and hospital.

Eli got a great picture of Olivia behind bars using her phone. Another tourist offered to take a pic of them together. Eli put his arm around her, pulling her close as they posed.

"Let me check those pictures, Olivia. The lighting isn't good in here." She waited while he checked them. "They're great." He thanked the man.

With his hand on Olivia's lower back, he guided her toward the area where the tortoises were waiting to be fed.

"Look at that big one. He has to be an antique." Olivia headed that direction while Eli purchased some food for the old tortoise.

"Here, Olivia. Get closer and feed him. Look at me and I'll get your photo while he chomps on the vegetables."

"Okay." She got down on one knee and leaned toward the head of the tortoise. "Is this close enough?"

"Perfect. Don't let him mistake your fingers for a carrot." He held the phone up for a picture.

"I didn't think of that."

Eli caught the worried look on her face when she jerked her fingers back. He checked the picture and laughed, then sent several shots to his phone.

"This is fun. You want to feed him?"

"And deprive you of the experience? Not on your life." Moving to the other side of the tortoise, he got another angle. He focused a close-up on Olivia's face, her lip gloss in the sunlight, her hair blowing in the gentle wind, her long lashes that fanned out perfectly on her cheek when she looked down. He wanted to look into her eyes forever. She was amazing inside and out, timeless, he decided, but time was slipping away. He needed to make a move. And fast.

CHAPTER 5

After boarding the weathered boat for their return trip to Zanzibar, Eli found them a bench seat with a great view and put his arm behind her, sending a comforting feeling through Olivia. The water was calm on the return trip to Zanzibar, which was good for Olivia's stomach.

"How are you feeling about this morning's attack? You okay?"

She sighed. "I may have nightmares and need serious counseling, but you've taken my mind off it."

"That was the plan." He hugged her briefly.

"I enjoyed our excursion." She smiled.

"I'm glad. But I've got to tell you something. I think that old tortoise had a crush on you."

"Why do you think that?" She turned a bit to see his face.

"He started following you when we left. You were just too fast for him, leaving him behind like that. You broke his heart."

"Maybe the tortoise was a female and she saw a hunky missionary taking her picture and couldn't resist. She didn't want to be left behind and had to chase you."

"I doubt that."

"What if you're the heartbreaker?" she asked.

He hesitated. "Are we still talking about a tortoise?" He turned and caught her gaze.

She bit her bottom lip and stared at the waves in the wake of the boat. "I bet Joy's last thoughts were about hating to leave you and Judah. I know mine would have been. It's not fair her life was snuffed out when you two were making such a difference on the island."

"You sound like you've been doing some research."

"Well, Happy did fill me in a bit. So many lives have been changed since your arrival. The church people understand your situation but hate to see you leave Zanzibar."

"They're former Muslims who have converted to Christianity. Most of them were born into Islam and didn't know there was any other way. I love them, but a great couple will replace me. It's time for me to go home." He paused. "I can't do this alone. I need to tie up some loose ends on the island and get my family stateside, then decide what to do next."

*****

Any questions about what type of wife he needed were answered. Olivia knew he needed a woman with a call to missions. That counted her out.

"Are you sad about leaving? You've invested so much into these people." She watched his expressions.

"It's always hard to close a chapter of your life. I'm leaving a lot of memories on this island. But things are heating up, and I've got to think about Judah's safety."

He stood and offered her his hand. "But for right now, it's time to get off this boat."

Once they were on the pier, Eli put her hand through his elbow and put his hand on hers. "How about a trip to the Zanzibar Butterfly Farm? It's about twenty kilometers south."

"Great idea. I'd love it."

They reached his SUV. He opened her door, then navigated the mixture of animals and vehicles on the road like a professional.

"Is it hard to drive here?" She hung on as he dodged a donkey.

"Not really, after you get used to driving a five-speed on the wrong side of the road with the steering wheel on the wrong side of the truck. Then it's just a matter of being aggressive enough to get your nose out there and alert enough to miss potholes and unpredictable animals who go astray."

They traveled in comfortable silence for a while. Olivia took random pictures as they traveled rough roads out of Stone Town.

"What's the name of this town.?"

"It's called Tunguu. Many people who work in Stone Town have their families living here. They visit on their leave times."

"This area reminds me of a village I've seen in Kenya, since there aren't any palm trees."

"I've been in a few parts of Kenya. Most of my travels have been in Tanzania and, of course, Zanzibar." Eli downshifted to slow the SUV and went off-road to pass a fender bender. "Hang on, this ride could get bumpy."

It already is. She grabbed the handle on the side of the SUV's windshield and hung on.

"We're here. It's full of beautiful specimens."

As they entered, the guide explained the farming process and the stages of a caterpillar-slash-butterfly life, before they entered a screened tropical garden where forty-six species of butterfly flittered about, displaying their gorgeous colors.

"Let me have your phone." Eli found the camera icon on her cell.

After Olivia put it in his hand, a beautiful black-and-white butterfly with turquoise patches on its wings landed on her arm. She froze while he took a picture.

"My turn." She took the phone and photographed an orange-and-black specimen on Eli's hair. She turned the phone and showed him the picture.

They walked past an area where cocoons were hanging in rows. Olivia took several photos of butterflies in various sizes and colors before giving him the phone again.

"Isn't God amazing? He planned this transformation." Olivia held another butterfly. "I love the white polka dots on the black wings."

"Yes, our creative God is awesome. Did you know that if we opened the cocoon for the butterfly and set it free, it would never fly? It must go through the struggle of getting out of the cocoon on its own to have strength in its wings to be able to fly." He took her picture as he talked.

"What an analogy. It's like the struggles we go through. If we do it God's way, we come out stronger for the experience. But that doesn't make the trials easy."

"Wow, I can attest to that."

A mass of small white butterflies flew past them. "They look like snowflakes."

Eli took a shot as a large colorful specimen landed on Olivia's shoulder. He looked at the screen. "I love that one. Send it to me."

He opened the exit for her.

"That was fun. What great pictures! I'm anxious to look at them."

"There's a gift shop. You want a framed butterfly to take home?" He led her toward the quaint little shop.

"Absolutely! I'll frame these pictures to hang with it."

Eli insisted on paying for her purchases and carried her packages, always the gentleman. "We're a bit early, but let's go to the restaurant. It's called the Rock, and there are only twelve tables. It's off-shore. We will drive back that same way we came, then we can walk there during low tide, but we will ride a small boat back to the shore when our dinner is over. People wait in line for as much as an hour for a table. The food is amazing."

"Sounds great to me."

After they drove back to Stone Town, Eli escorted her to the restaurant, stopping to buy some mixed flowers from a vendor on the sidewalk before they stepped onto the sand. "For you." He presented her with the bouquet.

"I love flowers. Thank you."

Reaching their destination, they climbed the steps to the small restaurant built on a rock. A waiter took their order. They settled back to wait at least an hour or longer for their entrees to be served. The fragrance of meats being grilled filled the area.

"The meat sure smells good, Eli, and this view of Stone Town is amazing." She took some pictures.

"It's worth the wait."

Olivia pulled a red-petaled flower from the bouquet. She plucked a petal from the stem and began rubbing it. Then another, making a pile of petals on the table as she talked.

"Why Zanzibar?" Eli took a drink of bottled water and sat back.

"I want to do more with my life than fly over the continent escorting tourists to great adventures. I've been interested in this island for a while. It seemed everywhere I turned, I kept seeing articles about Zanzibar. It felt like I was being led here for some reason. A couple of passengers were talking about the island on one of my flights. I began researching Zanzibar. My friends Jocelyn and Ellie and I have been talking about traveling and visiting some African countries while we're flight attendants."

"So they work with you?"

"Yes, and we share a condo in Kingwood, Texas. Ellie is interested in writing and photography. She wants to visit Timbuktu in Mali, West Africa, and try her hand at travel-writing for magazines. Jocelyn has a heart for the street children in Swaziland, South Africa. She wants to volunteer and possibly write grants to fund an orphanage there." Olivia finished with that flower and pulled another one out of the bouquet.

"Zanzibar sounded intriguing. I thought I'd like to be a tour guide, if given the opportunity. But after talking to Happy and Maria on my tours, I see that jobs are so scarce I'd be putting one of them out of a job if I applied. So I've changed my mind. And…"

"Your scary experiences with Aga Kahn have hampered your desire to live here. Don't get me wrong, Zanzibar is a great place to visit, but…"

They finished in unison. "I wouldn't want to live there."

Olivia smiled. "So I'll go back to the African skies and consider other possibilities."

"Does your father worry about your occupation?" He wiped the condensation off his water bottle.

She paused. "If he does, he's never mentioned it. His thriving company and country clubs keep him busy. A good golf game occupies his time off. I love him, but I haven't been a priority in his life since we lost Mom to cancer. I was in college, basically on my own, and my dad moved on without me. We spend holidays together, and he's good to me, but I miss the close, loving family we had before Mom got sick." Olivia depetaled another flower.

"Can I ask you something?" Eli looked at the pile of petals on the table, then met her eyes.

"Sure." She looked up.

"Why are you removing the flower petals?" He pointed to the pile on the tablecloth.

"I'm sorry." She put her hand on his and gazed into his eyes. "Please don't think that I don't appreciate your gift. I do more than most women would." She paused. "I was blind for seven years of my life, and I experienced life through touch, sound, and smell. I memorize life with my fingers. I capture the texture and scent of each petal when I feel of them. It was amazing to feel butterfly feet on my skin today."

"The Sahar of Zanzibar." He stared at her.

"Eli, why would you say that?" She tightened her hand on his. "Ali Baba called me that."

"But you forget the special meanings of the word. It means 'loyal, gifted, and enchanting.' I'm saying you're enchanting, Ms. Olivia Stone." He lifted her hand to his lips and kissed it. "If you run out of flowers, I'll buy you more." He winked.

"That's a deal." She raked the petals off the table and put them into the pocket of her jacket. "I hope you have a lot of money, Mr. Missionary." She laughed.

*****

"Fahad, did you implement my plan?" Aga Kahn paced the rooftop restaurant, where he met with his men over a meal.

Fahad stood to answer. "Yes. It was delivered this morning, as you instructed." He bowed before taking his seat.

"Touching Deckland's family will serve as a warning that his time in Zanzibar is coming to an end."

Zubair stood.

"Speak, Zubair," Aga demanded.

"The worker he calls Frances has been gathering boxes and packing the missionary's belongings. Your success is on the horizon, Aga Kahn." He bowed and took his seat.

"That makes me glad. Today may hurry his departure. We will see." He tossed enough shillings onto the table, then led the way to the exit. "Zubair, keep your eyes on the compound this evening and report activity to me immediately."

"Yes, Aga Kahn."

*****

After an amazing meal, Eli and Olivia returned to his truck. Before he cranked the vehicle, he noticed her staring at him. "What?"

"Can I memorize your face?" She spoke softly.

"Okay." He leaned toward her, coming face-to-face over the console.

"Now, close your eyes." She waited.

He complied. Olivia's feather-like touch started in the middle of his forehead and traced down the sides of his face to his chin. She smoothed his eyebrows, his eyes, and his cheekbones. She cradled the sides of his face before her fingertips brushed his lips. He opened his eyes and saw hers were shut as she concentrated. When she ended with the scruff of his afternoon shadow of a beard, he waited.

She opened her eyes slowly. "I will not forget."

"Now, it's my turn. Close your eyes."

Surprised, she paused, staring at him, but complied.

Eli leaned closer to her and traced her forehead, her eyes, and her cheeks with a gentle touch. He framed her face with his hands and brushed her lips with a tender kiss. Her eyes sprung open.

She sucked in a breath and stared with warring emotions on her beautiful face. "Were you kissing Joy or me, Eli?"

"Only you, Olivia." He captured her lips and kissed her with passion. When she relaxed into his embrace and twined her hands around his neck, he deepened the kiss, a kiss that demanded nothing but offered everything.

The ringing of his cell phone interrupted the moment. He pulled back, breathing heavily. "Olivia, hold that thought." He glanced at the display on his phone and looked up at her. "It's Frances."

He pushed her number. "Frances, what's wrong? Is Judah okay?" He cranked the truck as he listened. "Put him in his pajamas, fix his backpack with his cup and some snacks, and I'll be right there. Have John ready to open the gate." He ended the call.

"What wrong?"

"Judah's very sick. He's been having diarrhea, and his fever is high. It came on fast. We need to get him to the hospital." Eli had his flashing lights on and used his horn repeatedly, getting them there quickly.

John had the gates open. Frances waited on the porch with Judah in her arms. "Bwana, he acted like he didn't feel well this afternoon and wouldn't eat his dinner." She put the boy into Eli's arms.

Olivia felt Judah's forehead. "Frances, has he had a fever reducer?"

"Not yet. I waited for Bwana."

Olivia turned to Eli. "How far is the hospital?"

"Ten minutes. Will you hold him as I drive?"

"Sure." She got into the truck and opened her arms for Judah.

"Frances, I'll call you as soon as I know something." Eli slid into the driver's seat and drove as fast as the traffic would allow. When they reached the hospital, Eli wheeled in on two wheels and slammed the SUV into park by the emergency entrance. He took Judah and rushed into the hospital.

"Throw me your keys, Eli."

He did, and she attempted to move his truck into a parking space. It died once and jerked a few times, but she parked it without incident. She hurried into the sad excuse for a hospital. It was small, with antiquated equipment. *Lord, I have concerns about the quality of care this hospital can offer. Please touch Judah. You're his only chance of survival.*

*****

Aga Kahn reached for his cell phone but knocked it to the floor in the dark. He huffed as he grabbed the phone and opened it. "Kahn here."

"Aga Kahn, you asked me to inform you of activity at the missionary's home." Zubair waited.

"And?"

"Deckland retrieved the boy and has driven away with much speed. I assume he took him to the hospital." Zubair paused. "The worker did not accompany them. She must not have consumed any of the milk."

"Zubair, go home for the night. You have done your job."

"Yes, Bwana."

Kahn closed his flip phone and returned to his bed with a smile on his face.

*****

Eli was hovering over his son when Olivia rushed into the emergency part of the hospital. The old building showed wear but offered a bit of hope to the sick and wounded while assaulting them with an antiseptic smell mingled with the scent of a strong cleanser.

Judah looked so small lying on the long hospital gurney. Color had drained from Eli's face when she hurried to his side. "What did they say?"

"His fever is 102. A nurse is bringing some meds to bring that down. They're going to do some tests. The doctor mentioned typhoid as one possibility."

"Typhoid? Is there medicine for that?" Olivia's brows furrowed with concern.

"Yes, but he'll be a very sick boy for the first two to three days, then it will take a couple of weeks for him to be completely cured." He rubbed the hair off Judah's forehead. "It's okay, buddy. The doctor will help you feel better soon."

A Zanzibarian nurse with a tall stiff cap pinned to the top of her head approached the gurney. "Judah, I have some yummy juice for you."

Eli lifted him so he could drink the medicine.

"We have a place for him down this hall. You and your wife can follow me." She pushed the gurney past several curtained spaces and turned it toward the wall before pulling the curtain around them.

A lab tech entered. "Can you distract your son while we take blood?"

"Sure." Eli talked to Judah. "Hey, buddy, the nurse has to do a test. It won't take long. We need you to be brave. Okay?"

Judah watched Eli, probably too young to understand what he was saying but comforted by his voice.

Olivia looked in his bag and pulled out two matchbox cars and went to their patient. When they started the procedure, she held a car in front of his eyes. He smiled, reached for the car, then cried as a needle stuck him.

Eli had tears in his eyes. Olivia held Judah's hand and put her other arm around Eli's shoulder.

The nurse sent the blood to the lab, then took a stool specimen. She hurried away with the sample. Thirty minutes dragged by as they waited for a diagnosis. Judah dozed after his fever began to cool. Eli put his hand on Judah and closed his eyes. Olivia knew he was praying.

A Tanzanian doctor entered the curtained area and pulled the cloth closed behind him. He put his glasses on top of his head, pulled up a stool, and extended his hand to Eli. "I'm Dr. Waruri. Your son is very sick. It is typhoid, as we suspected. Nurses are bringing a dose of medicine for him now. They will give this dose every four hours through the night."

"Will he make it? He's only two." Eli rubbed the back of his neck.

"Yes, he'll survive. It was good that you got him to the hospital with haste. We'd like to watch him for twelve hours before allowing you to take him home." He stood. "Any questions?"

"How did he get typhoid?" Olivia wanted an answer.

"It's in his food or water. Is there anyone else sick at your home?"

Eli answered. "No, there's no one else with these symptoms."

"What has he eaten or drunk that only he consumed? It is there that you will find your answer." He moved toward the exit. "I'll check him again in the morning to make sure he's making progress. Then we'll release him into your care." The physician put his stethoscope into his coat pocket.

"Thank you, Dr. Waruri." Eli stood and shook his hand.

The doctor moved toward the curtain. "If anything changes through the night, I'm on call and the nurses will contact me." He slipped out of the area with a pull on the curtain.

Eli took his phone from his pants pocket and punched in a number. "Frances, it is typhoid, but he will live. We are staying at the hospital overnight."

He waited while she talked. Olivia could hear her praising the Lord.

"Frances, did you eat the same food as Judah today?" He listened and nodded to Olivia. "Did you drink the same things he drank today?" He waited. "Where did you get his milk?" His face showed concern. "Was it your regular delivery man?" He paced the room. "Do not drink it or let anyone else drink it. Do not pour it out. Tomorrow morning, go buy fresh milk for Judah." He listened to her. "Thank you for taking good care of him, Frances. You may have saved his life by calling me as soon as you did. Get some rest. The next few weeks will be busy with his care." He ended the call.

"What do you think?" Olivia put her hand on his shoulder.

Eli faced Olivia, his face angry. "It's a warning. Aga Kahn wants me out of Zanzibar."

"Has my presence brought on this attack? If I leave, will you and Judah be safe?"

He shook his head and grabbed her shoulders. "No, you can't go yet. It won't make a difference. Your resemblance to Joy put the target on your back, but that's not your fault. Aga Kahn has been trying to run me off the island since I arrived. His wife converted to Christianity in the first crusade that was held on the island. When she refused to renounce Christianity, she was killed for her faith. His anger still simmers. The success of my work threatens his stronghold."

"It scares me, Eli."

He opened his arms, and she walked into his embrace, a place she wanted to be held hostage for a long, long time.

*****

Being in this hospital resurrected bad memories for Eli as he rushed through the doors, smelled the smells, and waited behind these curtains. That same desperate panic gripped him. He took a deep breath and reminded himself that he served a God who heals.

As midnight approached, they moved Judah to a room, but he slept through transfer.

"His condition is improving." The night nurse tried to assure Eli. "He will be okay." She noted his temperature on his chart and lowered the bright lights to allow him to rest. "Are you two okay with the soft lights?"

"Yes. We're fine." He took a seat on the small couch by Olivia. "You want to take a taxi to the resort and get a good night's sleep?"

"I'm not sure I can sleep after this morning's attack and Judah's sickness. I'm afraid to try, if you want to know the truth." She slipped off her shoes and put her feet under her.

"What are your plans for tomorrow?"

"I've scheduled two days of sunbathing and lounging around the pool. I think I'll need a nap too. I assume you're staying home for the next few days."

"Yes, I'm staying close to Judah until I know he's going to be okay. He's a healthy kid, and I know the Lord will heal him."

"I agree. And I don't blame you for staying close. I hope you can catch a nap too."

"I'll attempt to rest while Judah sleeps." He ran his fingers through his hair. "I'm sorry we were interrupted. I stand with my prior assessment."

"What assessment was that?" A small smile threatened her lips.

"You're enchanting, Olivia Stone." He rubbed his finger down Olivia's cheek.

She stared at his eyes, savoring his touch. "It was a very special moment."

"I'd like an encore."

"I'm pretty booked up, but I'll check my schedule." She smiled.

"Mama."

Olivia jumped up and went to Judah's bed. "Hello, sweet boy. You feeling better?"

"Car?"

"His hands are empty, Eli. Help me find his cars. I gave him a blue car and a yellow truck."

They searched his covers. The yellow truck fell to the floor as they shook his blanket. Olivia retrieved it and put it in his chubby little hand. Eli found the blue car under his pillow.

Judah signed thank-you and smiled.

Eli gave him a drink from his sippy cup and rubbed his back until he went back to sleep.

Olivia eased away from the father-and-son duo and watched from her seat on the uncomfortable couch. As Eli lingered at Judah's bedside, her eyes got heavy. She leaned back and relaxed. And slept.

In the darkness of the chilly room, she felt Aga Kahn's hands around her neck. She couldn't breathe. Panic wrapped its bony fingers around her windpipe as his hands tightened. She struggled. Fought him. Smothered a scream.

Eli caught her arms. "Olivia, you're safe. It's just a bad dream."

Attempting to escape his hold, she jerked her arms.

"You're safe, Liv."

She opened her eyes, looked around the room, and stared at Eli as the truth dawned. "Oh, Eli. It was this morning's attack."

He put his arms around her trembling body and held her close to his chest as he prayed for peace. "Lord, the enemy comes to steal, kill, and destroy, but You are all-powerful, ever present in dark times. We need Your arms around us, protecting us and giving us peace as the storm rages on. Heal Judah for us, Lord. Give Olivia sweet sleep without interruptions. We trust You, Jesus. Amen."

CHAPTER 6

Under swaying palms and a cloudless sky, Olivia reclined and tried to relax, but a certain missionary invaded her thoughts. His touch was gentle for a man of such strength. He was a man's man, a hunk of a male specimen who ignored the heads he turned. Ellie would call him a catch.

"Would you like a soft drink?" A waiter cast a shadow, blocking the sun's rays. His presence pulled her out of her train of thought.

"Yes, a Coke with clean ice, please."

She watched some Zanzibaris fishing from their dugout canoe about twenty feet from the sand. This canoe was a bit bigger than the one she'd seen a few days before. These men had great success weighing down their rickety boat. It made her smile. Another family would eat tonight.

Her waiter delivered her soda and some cookies. "Thank you. Please charge this to my room."

He held her ticket and a Bic pen. "What number is it?"

"One zero seven." She took a sip, then realized her mistake—but he was already gone and she didn't see what he looked like. *Great private eye you are, Olivia, saying your room number out loud.* Ali Baba could be paying him to get that information. Great! Her day of rest just took a nosedive.

She took another drink of the cold soda and went to the edge of the waves to get her feet wet in the cool water. She put her hair into a messy bun with a scrunchie she had around her wrist and let the salty air cool her neck. With closed eyes, she memorized the experience. Pure peace.

Until a Zanzibari woman selling straw hats ran toward her, yelling, "Nyoka! Nyoka!"

Olivia turned and saw her motioning frantically for her to come out of the water. She hurried to the sand, then looked back to where a poisonous sea snake was slithering at the water's edge.

"Asante! Asante! Thank you so much for helping me." Olivia took the woman's hand and led her to the lounge chair where her bag lay. She reached inside and retrieved some shillings and put them in the woman's hand. "Asante, thank you."

The woman tried to refuse, but Olivia wouldn't let her return the money. She'd saved her life. The Zanzibari woman's toothless smile was calming to Olivia as the truth dawned. Danger had come close when she wasn't looking.

*****

Using the day at home, Eli made a follow-up call to the national children's department. "Children's Services, this is Eli Deckland. Can I speak to Emily Mungo?" He waited.

"Bwana Deckland, Emily Mungo here. How can I help you?"

"I wanted to get an update on my adoption of Rebecca Joy Mungaine. I've lived in Zanzibar long enough to meet the requirement to adopt a Zanzibari child. Becca is half-American. The father was a tourist who raped and assaulted my houseworker who has a serious heart condition. Giving birth to this child has taken all her strength. She will pass within the next few weeks. I need to apply for a passport for the baby girl. Your secretary, who took my application, asked me to call you today."

"I have reviewed your case, and your being an American makes you a great candidate for this particular baby. With you being the one she has chosen does sway things your direction as well. You have met the residency requirement. Do you have the financial request Parliament demands?"

"No. As a missionary in Zanzibar, I do not make that kind of money. Could I appeal for leniency? Would they make an exception since I've worked diligently to better the island? We have done feeding programs, beautification projects, and children's medical clinics."

"I will note that in your file and make that request on your behalf, but I can't make any promises." Ms. Mungo was all business.

"Do you have any timeline on the decision and finalization of this adoption? I'm moving to the States as soon as this is complete."

"As you know, I've been out of town until yesterday. I'll follow up on this right away and give you a call, Missionary Deckland."

"Thanks. That's all I can ask." He noted the date and what she said on his adoption file, then taped the bottom of another moving box. After the attack on Judah, he was ready to close this chapter of his life and start a new one, as a single father of two.

Eli stepped to the door between his bedroom and the living room. His houseworker was sweeping as she hummed. "Frances, how is Jessicah today?"

Frances put her hands on the top of the broom handle. "Bwana, she is getting weaker. She can no longer walk without my help."

"Just let her enjoy her baby as long as she can. Help with Becca when she needs to rest. It is all we can do for her." Eli worked on a roll of tape, trying to find the end.

"I am sad about Jessicah but happy our Judah is going to be okay. I was concerned." She took a tissue from her apron pocket and wiped her nose.

He put his hand on her arm. "I know you love him, Frances. And he loves you. I couldn't have made it after losing Joy if you hadn't helped me with Judah."

"You have been a blessing to my life. It will be good to be with my family, but I will miss you."

"And we will miss you, Frances. But you'll enjoy your grandchildren." He put some files in the box.

She wiped under her eyes with the corner of her apron. "Yes, they need me now."

"You're a blessing, Frances." He picked up some books and added them to the box. "So how about helping me pack this office?"

"Sure, Bwana."

*****

Dressed in a modest burgundy one-piece, Olivia left the beach to enjoy a lounge chair by the pool. As she got comfortable, her cell dinged with a message. She dug her phone out of her beach bag.

From: Jocelyn

Hey, you! Have you forgotten me and Ellie? We haven't heard from you. I hope that means you're having a wonderful time and getting the answers you're seeking.

Our schedule has changed. You have one extra day in Zanzibar if you want, or you can meet us at our hotel in Nairobi. Text your plans.

Love you,

J

Do I want to extend my stay? The trauma she'd experienced in Zanzibar resurfaced, sending her into a jumble of thoughts. *Aga Kahn scares me, but I'm not ready to leave Eli, but staying longer will make it harder to say goodbye. What am I thinking? Our occupations are complete opposites. I'm not a missionary. I can't give him more children. I'm not who he needs. It's hopeless.*

Her eyes welled with tears. She dabbed them with her beach towel and decided to answer Jocelyn later. Alerting the waiter, she ordered lunch, then reclined and watched some lovebirds on a tree limb near her while she waited.

"Thank you, Bwana." Her lunch was delivered to her poolside. It was a great presentation, with colorful condiments artfully displayed by her club sandwich and fries. A vervet monkey crept close, attempting to steal a bite. It made her smile.

Her waiter shooed the monkey away and stood close to keep him at a distance until Olivia finished. As the waiter removed her tray, her cell phone rang. She answered on the fourth ring. "Hello."

"Hello, Olivia. It's your dad. But I guess you saw that on your phone."

"No, I grabbed my cell quickly so I could catch this call." She paused. "You okay, Dad? You don't usually call me out of the blue, and it's the middle of the night there."

"Where are you, Olivia? Are you between flights?" He waited.

"No, I took a couple of weeks off. Sort of a vacation. I'm in Zanzibar. I fly to Nairobi in a few days, then I'll work the flights back to the States. I'll be in Texas again in seven days."

He breathed into the phone. "I have a health issue. Can we meet when you're back in Texas?"

"Sure, Dad. But tell me now. What is it? What's wrong?" She sat up straighter and covered her other ear with her fingers.

"It's my heart, Olivia. The cardiologist says I have at least three blockages, maybe four. I'm facing open-heart surgery after I take a round of antibiotics for bronchitis." He coughed several times. "Sorry."

"Have you been having issues, or did you have a heart attack?" Olivia waited.

After a pause, he spoke. "I didn't want to worry you." He coughed again. "It was a heart attack. I was on the golf course. Luckily, I had Doc Taylor on my team. He saved my life while my caddy called an ambulance."

"Are you in the hospital now?"

"No. After getting me stabilized on blood thinners, they released me to rest at home until you're here for the surgery. They'd like to schedule it for the end of next week."

"That's eight days. Why not have it sooner? Does this jeopardize your life by waiting?"

"He said I'll be fine if I lie low and get proper rest. This delay will give me time to take the antibiotics to clear bronchitis in my chest and time to instruct my team on pressing business matters. I need you to be home for this surgery." He paused. "Your mother handled health issues like a pro. I wish I were more like her. I'm not ready for this, Olivia."

"Dad, I'm glad you let me know. As soon as I land, I'll call you. You're going to make it through this. You know Mom would encourage you to rely on your faith in the Lord, to believe and have confidence in Him. That's been harder for both of us since she left us, but it's what we believe. It's who we are. You will come through this. I'll be with you."

"Thanks, Liv."

He hasn't called me Liv since Mom died. He's struggling.

"You're welcome, Dad. Please follow the doctor's instructions. Until next week, I'll be praying."

"I appreciate that. I love you."

She heard a break in his voice. *He's crying.* The line went dead. She stared at her cell.

*****

Eli paced his porch as he listened. "Ms. Mungo, does this mean I cannot adopt Becca? Her mother wants me to raise her."

"How does Parliament know those are her wishes? Did she write it down?"

Static interrupted the call. "Ms. Mungo, are you still there?"

"Yes, Bwana. Our connection is bad."

Eli continued the conversation, glad he didn't lose the call. "Jessicah has worked in my home for three years. Because of her heart condition, she has never attended school. She can't write." He understood her being thorough.

"Can she come into my office and tell me her wishes for her child?"

"She's too weak and probably has days to live. Could you come to my home, or would a video presentation be acceptable?" Eli tensed. This had to work.

"Let me come there later today, and if you can have a video camera ready, we will record her wishes for little Becca. I'll bring some documents she can mark."

"Thank you so much. If I left Becca in Zanzibar, she'll be bullied or abused because she won't fit in. She is a beautiful, light-skinned Zanzibari child with blue eyes."

"Let's put her in the video. It may help your case. I have your address. I'll be there in an hour. Is that okay, Mr. Deckland?"

"Absolutely, and thank you."

*****

"Hello, Aga Kahn. May I enter your home?"

"Officer Debano, sure. Come into the conference room. I'm just ending a meeting. Give my men a moment to leave." He stepped aside for the detective to enter.

Seeing Aga Kahn motion for them to leave, Fahad and Zubair bowed to their leader and eased out of the room.

"Tea, Officer?" He took a seat beside a table with an elaborate Indian-style tea set on it.

"No, but thanks. I just finished having afternoon tea with my officers." He took a seat at the conference table a few feet from Aga Kahn.

"To what do I owe this unexpected visit?" Kahn stirred sugar into his tea, appearing casual in his demeanor.

The detective opened his notebook and began reading a list. "You are aware that you and your men are suspects concerning Joy Deckland's death. That investigation is ongoing. The fire at the Christian church and the destruction of their security wall is under investigation as well. Your men are looking guilty of those crimes. You had Officer Gichuhi apprehend Ms. Stone, which is against protocol. My officer reported other criminal activity concerning threats to Ms. Stone and breaking into her room." He checked his notebook. "Another report was filed concerning you attacking Olivia Stone. We are scanning the surveillance tapes tomorrow to prove your guilt. And we suspect your men may have had something to do with the tainted milk delivered to Deckland's gate that made his son very sick. Deckland says he'll be in to see me tomorrow to press additional charges against you." He closed and pocketed his notebook. "This has to stop, Aga Kahn. You know the stand I've taken against violence on this island, and I will do that again if this persists."

"Detective, as you investigate, you will discover it is all circumstantial. My hands are clean. Deckland is realizing that it is time for him to leave the island. He is grasping at the straws they use in their sodas."

Debano stood and faced Kahn. "I'm warning you. The evidence is stacking up. Leave them alone. We rely on tourism as our greatest source of income on the island. With Olivia Stone being a flight attendant, she can hurt our reputation. I demand that you cease your attacks now. Let them leave Zanzibar, or this could end you. We have known each other for a long time, but a crime is a crime. I will not cover for you." He started toward the door. "It's time to back off, Kahn." He left him at the table.

When the door shut, Kahn poured himself another cup of masala tea, unfazed by the officer's visit.

*****

"Frances, how is Jessicah today?" Eli stood in the kitchen door, watching his worker prepare lunch.

"Very weak, Bwana. She cries a lot."

"It's sad. She doesn't want to leave Becca." He popped some grapes she had just cleaned into his mouth. "A lady named Emily Mungo is coming for a visit in a few minutes. She is from the Children's Services office and wants to talk to Jessicah and see Becca. Can you help her be presentable and get Becca dressed? Then prepare some tea, please."

"Yes, Bwana. Can you feed Judah until she arrives?" Frances dried her hands on a kitchen towel and put Judah's food on the table.

"Sure." He picked up his son, washed his hands, and fastened him into his chair at the table. "Ready to eat, little buddy?"

Judah clapped his hands. "Yeah." He took Eli's hand and bowed his head. Eli prayed over his food, and Judah grabbed a sliced grape and plopped it into his mouth when Eli said "Amen."

"So we have an appetite today." Eli watched as his son shoveled food into his mouth. "Hey, slow down there. Take a drink so you don't get choked." He held a sippy cup for him. Judah signed thank-you, took another bite, and pulled his favorite toy out of his pocket, a bright-red matchbox car. He ran it back and forth on the table while he chewed his food.

Eli heard their gates opening and a car pulling into their compound a few minutes before a knock sounded on the door.

Judah raised his hand. "Hi."

Eli let Ms. Mungo in and introduced her to Judah.

"What a handsome boy you have, Bwana. It's in your application, but I'd forgotten you have a son."

"Will that hurt my chances to adopt Becca?" Eli stared at her.

"No, it will help that you're an experienced father."

"One thing I've learned the hard way. You don't want to get too close to this one while he eats, or you'll be wearing his lunch." He smiled. "I'll get my worker to watch Judah while we visit with Jessicah and Becca."

"I'll visit with him while you get your worker."

*****

Eli knocked, then stepped into Jessicah's room. It was a simple space with the essentials for the Decklands' employees, usually better housing than they would have on their own.

"Ms. Mungo, this is Jessicah Mongaine. And this sweet baby is Becca, or Rebecca Joy."

Jessicah stepped forward a bit and extended her hand. "Thank you for coming to see me. I'm not able to go to town any longer."

She shook her hand and took a seat in a chair Eli brought near Jessicah's bedside. "I regret that your strength is fading. Your declining health has brought me here concerning the future for your daughter. May we record this time together?"

"Yes, Bwana Deckland can record it for us." Jessicah's voice was weak.

Eli mounted a tripod and positioned his video camera toward Jessicah and Mrs. Mungo. "The camera is on and recording your visit." He sat and played with Becca while they talked.

"For the recording, please state your name." Ms. Mungo read from a form she'd brought with her.

"I'm Jessicah Mongaine."

"Please state your birth date and place."

"I was told I was born in December, but I don't know the date. I was born here in Zanzibar."

"Normally we have the mother come to our office and fill out many forms to request a specific family to be allowed to adopt their child. Considering your declining health and inability to write, I have chosen to record your wishes for your daughter, Rebecca Joy. We will show your beautiful daughter on the video after we finish our interview." She opened another document she'd brought with her. "Jessicah, upon your death, who do you wish to take custody of your daughter?"

"Eli Deckland."

Eli smiled.

"Is it your wish for him to become her legal guardian or father?"

"Yes, it is. He is a good man. He'll love her and take care of her like he does his son. Becca would be in a Christian home. That is my wish." Jessicah was adamant.

"I have to ask this. Has he threatened or bribed you in any way to persuade you to give him your daughter?"

"No! He is a man of integrity who has treated me and Frances with respect. He would never do something like that. He has kept paying me and funding my doctor expenses even though I can no longer work for him and Judah."

"Jessicah, I am very sorry for your grave diagnosis." Ms. Mungo put her hand on Jessicah's arm.

"Thank you. I may have a few more weeks. Becca's smile makes me want to stay longer."

Mrs. Mungo had tears in her eyes when she turned to Becca lying on the floor on a blanket, playing with some blocks. "Hello, Becca."

The child handed her a block.

"Bwana, could you turn the camera on this beautiful baby girl?" She got on her knees on the floor by Becca.

Eli got Ms. Mungo and Becca centered in the frame.

She spoke into the camera as she lifted the baby and put her on her lap. "I am Ms. Emily Mungo, from Zanzibar Children's Services, and this is Rebecca Joy. Her mother calls her Becca. She is almost four months old. She's a blessing that came from a rape-slash-assault by an American tourist who left the island immediately after the incident. A serious heart defect experienced by Becca's mother has weakened her health during the pregnancy and birth of the child. The child is in perfect health, but as you can see, she is light-skinned and has bright-blue eyes. These physical attributes will make her life difficult on the island. The mother has requested that Eli Deckland, an American missionary here on the island, be given full custody of her child upon her impending death. Eli Deckland has met the requirement of living as a resident in Zanzibar for over a year." She returned the baby to the floor and glanced at the paperwork.

"About the substantial fee we require for adoption, I'd like to waive the fee in this case. Eli Deckland has incurred all the medical bills for Jessicah Mongaine. He will be paying for the burial expenses. He is preparing to leave Zanzibar permanently. He will have to pay for her passport, her plane flights, and all supplies for the child."

She picked up Becca again, holding her close to the camera. "This baby's future is in our hands. Can we pass this responsibility to Eli Deckland by allowing him to be her father legally?"

She motioned for Eli to step closer, then put Becca into his arms in front of the camera lens. Becca smiled. "I move for this to be approved with no delay. Thank you."

Eli used his free hand to turn the camera off.

Mrs. Mungo turned to Jessicah. "I wish you many more days with your sweet child. I'll do my best to see that your wishes are granted for her future. Goodbye, Jessicah."

She spoke to Eli. "I'll keep you updated on this venture. Could I speak with you for a minute?"

"Sure." He followed her out, with Becca in his arms. They talked as they walked to the front door of his home.

"What happened? You said she was raped. Could you give me some details, in case I'm questioned by members of Parliament?"

Eli paused. "My late wife, Joy, took Jessicah to the market. My wife was kidnapped, stabbed, and left at my gate. I rushed her to the hospital, but she didn't survive. Jessicah had to walk home alone in the rain. As darkness fell, an American tourist saw her, dragged her into an alley behind a building, and raped her. With her heart condition, she was too weak to fight him off. I'm sure he left the island the next day. Our neighbor found Jessicah and brought her home. Frances took care of her while Judah and I took Joy's body home for burial."

"I'm so sorry. What a sad story."

"Yes, it is. But it brought us to where we are today with Becca. I appreciate your help, Ms. Mungo."

"After seeing her, I know this adoption has to go through." She touched Becca's cheek. "I will call you."

"I pray blessings on you for all you do for the children in Zanzibar." Eli opened the front door for her.

She turned back toward Eli. "Someone has to speak for them. I'm glad to do it. I hope this adoption goes through for you. Have a good afternoon, Bwana." She pulled out of the compound and into the traffic, headed for the business district of Zanzibar, to continue her fight for children in Zanzibar.

CHAPTER 7

Olivia paced her hotel suite, trying to decide what to do about her dad. He never needed her. Never asked anything of her. *I need to get home.*

She grabbed her phone and texted a message to Jocelyn.

> Jocelyn,
>
> Is there an earlier flight that I can work to get me home sooner? My dad is having surgery, and I need to get stateside.
> Let me know.
>
> Thanks,
> Liv

She pressed Send and breathed a prayer for her dad. With a beautiful sunset displaying its splendor from her window, she decided a walk on the beach would calm her angst. After donning some lightweight linen pants and her flowered blouse, with sandals in her hand, she folded up the hem of her pants and let the waves wash over her feet. The cool water was refreshing in the tropical heat as a late-afternoon breeze cooled her skin. She bent down and scooped a handful of sand into her palm. *God, Psalms tell us that Your thoughts outnumber the grains of sand on the seashore. As You remember me today, please be with my dad and help me with Eli. Our lives are too different to combine. Give me wisdom, Lord. I trust You.*

The vibration of her phone changed her focus. She stood and faced the ocean. "Hello."

"Olivia, it's Eli. I'm just checking on you. You've been on my mind. You okay?"

"Yes and no. I'm safe. Thankfully, Ali Baba hasn't been around."

"But you sound sad. What's up?"

"It's my dad. He's having open-heart surgery at the end of next week. He never reaches out to me, but today he said he needed me. He called me Liv, a nickname he hasn't used since my mom died."

Eli's breath hitched. "Are you leaving early?"

"I don't want to. With my schedule as it stands right now, I'll be home in time for the surgery, but I texted Jocelyn to see if there's a flight I could work that would get me home sooner. I haven't heard from her yet."

"Wow. That sounds serious."

"For him to call me, I know it is. He's on bed rest until the surgery. He requested time for me to get back to the States and for him to prep his staff to handle things while he recuperates." She paused. "I'm sure he's meeting with his lawyer, updating his will, and making plans in case he doesn't make it. But he would never tell me that."

"I'm sorry, Olivia. That puts enormous stress on your shoulders. Do you have any extended family that can help?"

"Aunt Jana Rose, my dad's sister, will be there in the waiting room with me, giving me advice and encouragement, and she'll stick around and cook amazing food, whatever I need at the moment. She's pretty great. But don't mess with her. She's a take-the-bull-by-the-horns kind of woman, a beautiful blonde full of grit and grace."

"She sounds like a good aunt to have. I'd love to meet her."

"She can be handy in a pinch." Olivia smiled. "Sorry to dump my problems on you. Is Judah okay?"

"He's feeling better and is beginning to eat again. I called to make sure you're safe."

"I am safe and enjoying relaxing in this beautiful resort."

"I'm glad. The snow-white sand and turquoise waters are pristine. Enjoy your day tomorrow, Olivia. I had another reason to call. Would you like to visit the Forodhani Market Sunday evening? I'm staying here with Judah tomorrow, then preaching Sunday morning, but my evening is free. We could shop some, then have dinner. It's a Zanzibari highlight you don't want to miss."

"It sounds like fun. Sure, let's do it." She smiled.

"Can I pick you up at six?"

"I'll be waiting."

*****

Olivia enjoyed a marvelous Sunday-morning breakfast, then donned a sundress and sandals. Grabbing her floppy hat, she walked to the lobby and requested a taxi. The manager called one for her and bade her farewell.

"Take me to the Christian church on the outskirts of Stone Town, Bwana. I want you to park near the church, but I want to stay in your cab and listen without entering the church."

"Yes, Dada. We can do that. It will be a big rate. That okay?" He waited before leaving the resort.

"Do not worry about the cost. I will pay for it."

"Asante, Dada." He smiled and pulled them into the flow of traffic.

Even on Sunday morning, these people worked their kiosks and roasted sausages and ears of corn along the edge of the potholed roads. Olivia enjoyed their friendly banter, as they seemed happy with their lot in life. Simple people enjoying small pleasures.

"Bwana, park close enough so we can hear but not be seen."

"Yes, Dada." He parked by the security fence behind the church.

"This is perfect." She could hear and enjoy the Zanzibarians singing praises to the Lord. They were energetic and really, really loud. When Eli started preaching, he had an interpreter putting his words into Swahili, which made his sermon twice as long. He announced the death of one of their older members who'd had malaria.

"Death is a part of our lives. We will all die one day. In the Bible, in the book of Ecclesiastes 3, the scripture says, there is a time for everything and a season for every activity under the heavens. A time to be born and a time to die. As a church, we will celebrate the life of our friend who died and mourn our great loss. But let's also be reminded that one day we will pass from this life too. Our focus must be on keeping our sins washed clean and our hearts devoted to Jesus as we witness to others about His saving grace. There is one thing better than going to heaven." He paused. "It is taking someone with you."

The people clapped and gave tribal cries at that point, expressing their agreement.

When the noise died down, Eli continued. "It is important to remember our loved ones we have lost in death and continuously rededicate ourselves to sharing the good news with the lost around us. We have all been called to seek and save the lost."

Olivia's admiration of Eli grew as he spoke lovingly to his congregation, but it also confirmed her train of thought. *He needs a woman called to ministry as his wife, not a flight attendant who travels most of the time.*

"Bwana, you can take me back to the resort now."

He cranked the taxi and headed back toward the beach resort. After they'd traveled a while, he cleared his throat. "I listen to the man. Do you think he says the truth?" Traffic was light on this Sunday afternoon.

"Yes, he's a man of God, and he speaks the truth. If you turn from the ways of Allah and accept Jesus as your Savior, you will become a Christian, and when you die, you will go to live in heaven."

"I have not heard this before. It makes me feel different inside." He dodged some stray dogs as he took a roundabout.

"Bwana, that feeling is the Lord inviting you to become a Christian." Olivia met his eyes in the rearview mirror. "It is the truth, Bwana."

"Your God would want me?" He pulled the cab into the resort parking lot and stopped at the entrance to the lobby.

"Yes. He loves you so much." She waited.

"I need to talk to that man." He got out and opened Olivia's door.

She put her floppy hat on as she got out of the cab. "He will be here at six. Come back and you can talk to him."

"Asante, Dada."

*****

"Aga Kahn, I tried to call you earlier. I was near Olivia Stone in the lobby. She was talking to the lady at the desk. She is going to the Forodhani Market with Deckland. He is picking her up in thirty minutes." Fahad waited in the shadows.

"That delays our plan. We will execute the abduction after she returns to her room. You stay there and keep watch. Have Zabair follow them, keep his distance, and let me know when she is returning to the resort. We will be ready."

"One more thing, Aga Kahn." Fahad spoke cautiously.

"What is it?" Kahn waited.

"Officer Debano is having dinner here at the resort."

"Has he approached Olivia Stone?"

"No, Bwana. Just looking around."

"Did he see you watching her?"

"I do not think so," Fahad said.

"Not to worry. He will be gone before we take care of our business. Watch for his departure, Fahad."

"Yes, Aga Kahn. I will keep you informed."

*****

"Good evening, Olivia Stone. Who is this?"

"Eli, this is my new friend, Ahmad. He drove me to your church this morning, and we listened to your sermon. He wants to ask you about Jesus." Olivia looked at Ahmad and smiled.

Eli's eyebrows shot up. "Really. I'm always happy to share the good news. Hello, Ahmad."

Olivia knew Ahmad was nervous. "Eli, why don't you two take a seat in the lobby? I'll sit over here and return a couple of texts from my friends Ellie and Jocelyn. Take your time."

Eli and Ahmad talked for a while, then Eli put his hand on Ahmad's shoulder as he prayed with him. When they stood, Eli embraced the former Muslim. Olivia knew that was her cue to join the men.

After Ahmad left, Eli opened the door of his SUV for Olivia, then took a seat behind the wheel. "That was a pleasant surprise."

"I thought you'd enjoy it." She smiled and fastened her seat belt.

"Another name in the Lord's Good Book always makes me happy." He pulled the truck into evening traffic and just missed a collision with a donkey who was running from his master.

"That was close!" Olivia squealed.

"It's amazing there aren't more wrecks and injured animals in Zanzibar. Defensive driving is crucial."

"Okay, Mr. Tour Guide, tell me about this market." Olivia was glad to be with Eli again.

"It's called Forodhani Gardens. It is in Stone Town, along the sea walk. That quiet stretch of beach comes alive when the sun goes down. It's a unique street food experience. Chefs bring out their best. It's where the locals go for dinner to keep from cooking at home. You'll love it."

"Well, I'm game. It sounds like running through a drive-through in the States. But you choose our food. I don't want to eat something I shouldn't."

"It's a deal. You've got to try the sugarcane juice and Zanzibar pizza as an appetizer. Then we will shop for a while and find another vendor for our dinner meal."

After they parked the SUV at a church in Stone Town, Eli took Olivia's hand and led her to the sea walk. He stopped at a kiosk and got them some sugarcane juice.

"Here, try this."

She took a drink. "That's good. It's not as sweet as I thought it would be. But I like it."

They sat and enjoyed their juice, enjoying the hubbub. Zanzibaris were diving off some cliffs at the end of the beach, putting on quite a show as the sun went down. Dhows passed along the horizon in the distance. Locals were grilling skewers of meat, calamari, and lobster. The smell of pita bread wafted toward them.

Olivia loved the setting. "You were right. This is amazing. Thanks, Eli."

"Now, for that appetizer." He went to a friend and bought a plate of pizza and one Coke. He held it up. "I hope you don't mind sharing. It's the only thing cold, but I got two straws."

"I don't mind." She would memorize these moments. They perched on a ledge away from the chaos and ate.

"It's not like any pizza I've ever eaten, but it's good. Is this a fried egg in the middle of the pizza?"

Eli smiled. "Yes, between the crepe-like crust is beef, mayo, vegetables, and egg." He wiped his mouth. "Just like Pizza Hut. Right?"

"I don't think so." She took another bite.

He held their Coke toward her so she could drink.

"Thanks." She put her hand over his to steady the bottle. Warmth ran up her arm—his touch was electric.

"Did you have a relaxing day today?" He took a drink before putting their Coke on the ledge.

"I enjoyed your sermon this morning. You're really good. Do you know that?" She paused, thinking of the truth she realized listening to him. "I relaxed under a thatched umbrella and read most of the afternoon. But yesterday had its challenges. A monkey tried to steal my lunch, and I was standing at the edge of the waves when a Zanzibari woman yelled nyoka and got me back on the sand as a poisonous snake swam by."

"Those sea snakes are vicious, Olivia. I'm glad she warned you." Eli stopped eating and faced her. "I'm relieved you're okay."

"Me too."

He took a small bite of pizza crust and swallowed. "So when you add in the recent call from your dad, you did have a challenging day."

"But the weekend is ending well." She smiled at him.

Vendors carried their wares from tourist to tourist, trying to make a sale. Olivia ignored them until she saw something she wanted.

"I want some of those bracelets made from coconut shells and those that are slices of cow horns. My friends would like them." Olivia watched as the vendor came closer.

Eli motioned for him to approach. "The lady wants to see what you have."

"Okay, Bwana." He offered his merchandise.

Olivia picked three bracelets made of coconut shells and three that were slices of cow's horn. Then a wooden bracelet caught her eye. It had an intricate carving of an African scene around it. "This would be perfect for my aunt." She looked at the young man. "Bei gani, how much?"

"Ten dollars each," he said.

"Gali Sana, too much." She started putting them back. "Two dollars is enough."

"Give me five."

"No. Three is my best price." She stood her ground.

He paused, looked between Eli and Olivia. "Okay. Bring money."

She paid him and accepted the bag.

"You're a pro at this. I thought you'd need my help." Eli joked.

"I do. Someone has to carry my heavy bags." She handed him her small purchases.

"I don't think these bracelets are going to weigh me down."

"But I'm not done yet."

"Well, Ms. Shopaholic, let's see what we can find. There are some shops still open. What would you like to buy?"

"A T-shirt, some spices, and three brass trunks."

"What?"

"A tourist on one of my flights bought some brass trunks here on the island and shipped them home. I want some."

"Okay." They walked a few blocks, and Eli stopped. "Stay right here."

Olivia watched Eli speaking to a food vendor. The man got quite animated when giving directions.

Eli returned, took Olivia's hand, and led her down a cobblestone alley. "Olivia, step back toward the wall."

She complied, and her breath caught when three men passed with a dead python, a big one. "Where are they going with that snake?"

"I'm not sure but didn't want to ask." He pulled her hand to get them walking again. They turned a corner and stopped at one of those ornate Zanzibar doors with intricate carvings and iron stakes that had been added years ago to keep horses and elephants away in wartime. Eli knocked on the door.

It took a few moments, but the door creaked when it opened.

"Joseph sent me. My friend wants to buy a brass trunk. He said you had the best ones."

The man looked at Olivia, then stepped back, allowing them to pass. Once inside the dim room, he turned on the lights to reveal probably twenty brass trunks in various sizes.

Olivia ran her hand over the surface of the closest one. "Yes, these are wonderful." She went from one trunk to another, then turned to Eli.

"Ask him the prices for me, Eli."

Eli turned to the man and bargained with him in Swahili for a few moments.

"Which one do you want, Olivia?"

She smiled. "I want three of these in graduated sizes so they can fit inside one another and ship as one unit." She walked to the first one she touched. I want this one and two that will fit inside of it. Can you get me a good price and ask about shipping costs?"

"Okay. You sure?" he asked.

"Absolutely."

He looked at the shop owner and began his negotiations, then held his hand up. "Olivia, he's asking one hundred dollars for the big one, seventy-five for the medium-size trunk, and sixty for the smaller one. Is that okay?"

"Tell him two hundred dollars for all three." Olivia put her hands on her hips.

Eli told him. He shook his head no.

"Tell him two hundred and twenty-five dollars."

Eli relayed the message.

The man looked at Olivia and smiled. She had a deal. She stuck out her hand, and he shook it.

Eli took out a piece of paper and gave it to Olivia. "Write your name and address down, shopping queen." He smiled. "You made yourself a deal."

She was so excited she hugged Eli then took the paper and started to write. "Jocelyn and Ellie are going to love these."

*****

The feel of Olivia in his arms stole his breath. He stood watching her write her address for shipping. It gave him time to process what just happened.

"Is this all he needs, Eli?" Olivia showed the address to him.

Eli asked the shop owner a question.

"They will want your phone number too."

She added that to the list of information, handed Eli the paper, and took the money out of her purse. She folded the bills and gave them to Eli. "Will you pay him for me?"

"Sure." He paid for their purchase, then led Olivia out of the showroom, giving a farewell greeting to the shop owner as they left.

Olivia clapped her hands. "I'm happy with my purchases. My friends are going to be thrilled. How long will it take until they arrive?"

"Probably three weeks to a month."

"Perfect. I'll fill them with their Christmas presents and put them by our tree with huge bows."

"So you're a gift giver?" He motioned for her to walk back through the alley.

"I love to make people happy."

"Well, you've put a smile on my face. You were like a kid in a candy shop." He put his hand on her shoulder as they moved back into the crowd of tourists.

"It was fun."

They shopped at various kiosks as they strolled toward their dinner destination. Eli carried packages of T-shirts, spices, and a carved replica of a Zanzibari door.

"How about some dinner? We're having baked fish, potato balls, nans, and samosas."

"I'm ready. Lead the way." He took her hand again and led her to a quaint restaurant in the heart of the market. After they were seated, he ordered for both of them. "I'll get you a Coke of your own this time."

"Now you're splurging?"

"Only the best for you, shopping queen." He winked.

Their conversation returned to the shiny gold-colored trunks she'd purchased. "You made good choices among the brass trunks. Is there something else you want to buy in Zanzibar?"

"No, I'm good. Unless I can find a chess set for my dad."

"Do you want carved wood, soapstone, or quartz?"

She thought for a minute. "I think I'd like carved wood with the wood grain showing in the pieces."

"I know just the place. But it's not in Stone Town. When are you leaving the island?"

"Unless I can get another working flight, I have three more days." She sighed.

He let out a breath he didn't realize he was holding. "I can go by there tomorrow and let you know what he has in stock."

"Please don't go out of your way. I've taken so much of your time already." She reached for his hand.

"And I've enjoyed every minute." He rubbed his thumb over the back of her hand on the table. "Olivia, I'm not anxious for you to leave."

"Oh, Eli. I've grown fond of you too—"

"I hear a 'but' coming." He interrupted her.

"Our lives don't mesh, Eli. I'm not what you need. Trust me. You're a handsome catch someone is going to snatch up in no time. She will give you the future you deserve."

Their food was delivered, and he asked the Lord to bless it. They started eating without conversation.

"Another great choice. I love these samosas. I wish I could buy these in the States."

"I'll miss them when I go home." He put his fork down, letting it clang against the plate. "So you think I'm handsome?" The corners of his mouth threatened a smile.

"Yes, I think you're ruggedly handsome, Eli."

"Well, Ms. Stone, you're a beautiful woman. Why do you say you're not what I need? I think you're exactly who I need."

"As I listened to you preach this morn, I knew I didn't fit the bill. You need a missionary wife, a woman to stand beside you as you minister to the masses. And don't you think it's risky to have feelings for someone who looks like your late wife? Won't that make life awkward with your family and friends?"

"I see you as Olivia. Not Joy. You're nothing like her. And I don't care what they think. It will only be an initial shock. Once they spend time with you, they will see you for who you are."

She held his gaze, the candlelight highlighting the gold flecks in his amber eyes. "Our food is getting cold."

"Great segue."

They ate in amenable silence. Eli ordered flan for their dessert.

"Let me ask this again, Why do you think you're not what I need? We have great chemistry. We enjoy each other's company. Judah chooses you too. You know that."

"But isn't that deceiving him? I'm not his mother, Eli."

He reached over and rubbed between her eyebrows. "You furrow your brows when you're concerned." He sat back. "I agree, we need to sort out a few things, but I think there's more you're not telling me. So what is it?'

Olivia took a flower out of the bouquet on the table. She pulled the petals off one by one, feeling its smoothness, memorizing its texture and scent. She looked at Eli with tears filling her eyes. "I got sick when I was sixteen and had to have surgery. I can't have children. I'm incomplete, Eli." She held up her hand. "Don't say anything. Just try to understand."

Their flan was delivered along with two cups of hot tea. They ate in silence, as if in their own little bubble, as tourists milled about and hawkers sold their wares.

"This is a perfect ending to the flavors I've tasted tonight. It's so soothing to the palate." She put sugar in her tea.

"Do you analyze flavors too?"

"Food, flowers, music, and people." Her gaze took in his handsome face.

He paid their bill, pulled her chair out for her to stand, and leaned in. "I think you're overthinking this thing between us, Olivia." He put her hand in the crook of his arm and escorted her to his SUV. "It's getting late. Let's get you back to the resort."

As Eli pulled into the flow of traffic, a message came through on Olivia's phone. She took it out, read the message, texted a reply, and put her phone away.

"No earlier flights for me. I'm staying on my original schedule."

"I would say I'm sorry, but I'm an honest man." He laughed.

When they arrived at her hotel, he pulled into a parking place instead of the drive-through, where the valet waited to open her door.

"Are you wanting to show me how valiant you are by opening my door?" She clicked the button on her seat belt.

He reached over and pulled her toward him. "There is something great happening here, Olivia. You can't deny the sparks between us. This doesn't happen every day. Don't throw this away."

"But—"

He stopped her with a passionate kiss.

She eased her hands around his neck and melted into his embrace, overwhelmingly tempted to never leave his arms.

When he pulled back, he held his forehead to hers. "There is a Swahili proverb here in Zanzibar that says, 'A letter from the heart can be read on the face.' I see passion in your eyes. I feel it in your kiss. We can make this work. Give us a chance, Olivia Stone." He put his fingers on her lips so she couldn't respond. "Sleep on it, okay?"

"Okay."

He opened the truck door, walked her to her room, and kissed her again.

"Thank you for a wonderful evening."

"You're welcome." He kissed her forehead. "Good night."

"Night, Eli."

Once her door was shut, he returned to his SUV. *Please don't break my heart, Olivia.*

CHAPTER 8

"Asim, take me to the Dream of Zanzibar Resort." Aga Kahn got comfortable in the black luxury SUV.

"Yes, Bwana." He cranked the vehicle and pulled into the traffic flow.

The tropical heat of the day had been eased by an evening breeze. Aga Kahn watched the busy sidewalks filled with Zanzibari residents selling fruits, vegetables, and handmade items as they drove about the island. From the comfort of his SUV, Kahn planned the eradication of the threat to his authority. *Zanzibar will thank me.*

A shrill ring tone interrupted his musings. "Yes, Aga Kahn here."

"Aga Kahn, this is Fahad. Detective Debano has left the restaurant, and Olivia Stone has returned to the resort. Deckland walked her to her room, then returned and drove away."

"We are on our way. Do you have the master key?"

"Yes, Aga Kahn. I have everything you requested. We are ready. I await your instructions."

"Wait for me at the end of the parking lot, where the trees darken the area. We will make our move when Zubair arrives."

"I will be there, Aga Kahn," Fahad said.

Kahn ended the call and pocketed his phone. They were nearing the Dream of Zanzibar Resort. He smiled.

"Asim, drive to the far end of the parking lot. Back the SUV into the parking space. We will wait there for my men. We have a job to do. Be ready to leave immediately when we return."

"Yes, Aga Kahn. I will be ready."

Fahad was waiting in the shadows. He slipped into the vehicle. "Habari, Bwana. Hello."

"Have you talked to Zubair?"

"Yes, Aga Kahn. He is not far away, but there is a traffic jam because of an accident. Police are clearing it now."

"We will wait. We need his help. He is strong."

*****

African nights were raven-black, especially when the skies were overcast, as heavy clouds threatened rain. Olivia slipped into her pajamas after draping her clothes over a chair. Weary after the day, she climbed into bed and turned off the lamp. Lightning in the distance flickered a light show on the walls of her room, followed by rumbles of thunder. Soon the rhythm of rain tap-danced Morse code patterns on the roof. She fell asleep thinking of Eli's warm embrace and his passionate good-night kiss.

Thunder woke her, but she kept her eyes closed as the clean fragrance of rain filled the air. After a burst of thunder, closer this time, she sensed a presence in her room. She stilled and listened. When there was no sound, she relaxed again.

With intense force, a cloth was placed over her mouth by a large strong hand. She struggled to get out of his grasp, but breathing in a sweet smell, she lost her battle as she faded into a dark abyss.

*****

"She's out. Fahad, grab her clothes and shoes. Zubair, carry her. Let's move." Aga Kahn looked out and checked the area before he led the way.

Zubair lifted Olivia's limp body, threw her over his shoulder, and followed Aga Kahn into the rain.

Fahad was right behind them, hidden by the dark shadows of the tree line that bordered the resort property. They passed down an alley to the far end of the parking lot, where Asim waited in the running SUV. Fahad opened the back of the truck for Zubair to lay Olivia Stone on the carpeted floor. Before he closed the rear door, he tossed her clothes and shoes in beside her sleeping body.

*****

Olivia woke slowly as they bumped along on potholed roads. She felt dizzy and slightly nauseous. *Chloroform. They drugged me. Aga Kahn again.* When she realized she'd been kidnapped, she remained still, faking slumber. *He plans to kill me this time.* She listened for any clue as to where they were taking her.

Aga Kahn dictated instructions to his men. "Fahad, when we arrive, I'll get the key to the pool house from the main office. It hasn't been used for a while, but it will do for our purposes. Since you've been there before, you lead the way through the gardens. Zubair will carry Olivia Stone from the vehicle to the pool house. We have had success thus far. This will be over by midday tomorrow."

"Yes, Bwana. Do you want me to lock it and bring you the key?" Fahad asked.

"Yes, after you gag her and tie her hands and feet. We need her to stay quiet."

"We will do as you say, Aga Kahn." Fahad sounded resigned.

They traveled about fifteen minutes up an inclined road. Olivia felt the truck slant as it traversed the hill. The crashing waves of high tide let her know they were near the ocean.

"We will have our regular meeting in the morning here in my seaside villa. I will be ready to begin at nine. You two come, and if you can find him, bring Usama with you. We must deal with his failure with Joy Deckland. After the other employees leave, we will deal with this problem once and for all."

*****

Hearing the back of the truck open, Olivia kept her eyes closed. The big guy picked her up and put her over his shoulder again, as if she were a sack of potatoes.

"Fahad, grab her clothes, shut the truck, and open that gate." Kahn moved toward the front door of his mansion.

Fahad retrieved her shoes and clothes, brushed some debris from the back of the truck onto the driveway. He slammed the door and hurried to retrieve the key and to open the gate.

Olivia felt stems and leaves touching her arms as they hung limply at the man's back. She opened her eyes to a slit and saw an array of gorgeous flowers. She grabbed several flower heads and quickly depetaled them as they went toward the pool house. When they stopped for Fahad to open the door, she grabbed one more bloom and hid it in her tight fist.

"Put her on the bed. I'll get something to use as a gag. Aga Kahn said there was some rope in the cabinet under the sink. We can use it to tie her hands and feet."

They worked together and had her bound and gagged in no time.

Once the goons left, Olivia turned over to survey the forgotten room, its musty smell assaulting her nose. There was one opened louvered window that could offer a reprieve from the tropical heat. *Hopefully, the rain will cool the temperature tomorrow. That's a stupid thought. I'm worried about the temperature when I'm about to be murdered. I should have left on the first ferry off this island. But no! I ignored the threats. Look where it got me! And no one knows I'm missing.*

Her ankles were too tight for her to get free, but her wrists were a bit looser. She had clenched her fists, giving her some leeway when she relaxed her hands. She worked on them until her skin was raw, but soon her hands were free. She jerked the gag from her mouth and rubbed her swollen lips. Their roughness had split her upper lip in two places. She looked for the flowers she'd kept in her fists when lightning lit up the room. She depetaled them, hopped across the room, and put the petals on the window ledge. *I hope Eli has read the nursery rhyme about leaving a trail of bread crumbs. It's my only hope of getting out of here alive.*

*****

Eli was at the resort by eight o'clock in the morning. He couldn't wait. He had to talk to Olivia, had to finish their conversation.

Knowing she usually ate around eight thirty, he asked which table was hers and waited for her arrival. He sipped a cup of Kenya AA Blue Mountain coffee, some of the best in the world, while he waited. At nine o'clock, he began to get anxious and went to the front desk and spoke to the receptionist.

"Excuse me, I've been waiting for Olivia Stone for some time. I'm concerned. Would you bring a key and go with me to her room?"

The manager overheard his request. "I will accompany you."

"Thank you." Eli followed Paul Kamau, the manager, to Olivia's door.

"Her door is open just a bit." He looked at Eli. "Ms. Stone, are you in there?"

"Olivia! I'm coming in." Eli pushed the door open. "She's gone. Call the police." He started looking for clues. He found her purse with her passport inside. Her camera was still in its case.

"Are you sure she isn't at the beach? Maybe she took an early-morning walk to collect shells," Kamau said.

"And leave her passport, purse, and camera? I don't think so." Eli held up her purse and showed him the passport.

The manager called security and the police. "Don't touch anything. Maybe they left fingerprints. The heavy rains of last evening have washed away any footprints on the sidewalks."

Panic seized Eli. *Lord, help me find her before it's too late.* He took a deep breath and sighed. "She would never leave her passport behind. Americans guard it with their life when they travel." He checked the windows. "All the windows are locked from the inside."

"They had to use a key. I had an employee quit suddenly yesterday afternoon. He said he was offered a job with larger pay. He may have had something to do with her disappearance."

"Be sure to report that to the police so he can be questioned." Eli could hear sirens in the distance and sat in the chair by the door to wait for their arrival and called Detective Debano.

"Detective, Olivia Stone has been kidnapped. Aga Kahn has gone too far this time."

"Sorry, Deckland. I heard the call on the radio. I'm on my way."

Eli could hear his police siren as he ended the call. With his elbows on his knees, he leaned forward and put his face into his hands and prayed silently while the manager reported their suspicions to his security guards. Eli clasped his hands in front of him and stared at the floor. When the manager ushered Officer Debano and several police officers into the room, a breeze blew some wilted flower petals across the floor.

"Purple flower petals." He stood as he inspected the floor.

"What, Bwana?" Kamau asked.

"Olivia loves to take the petals off flowers and feel their softness. She did that at dinner last night and put the petals from several flowers in her pocket. If they took her out of bed, her clothes were probably on this chair. When they grabbed her clothes, the petals fell out of the pocket." Eli looked around the room. There were a few petals by the door. He stepped out of the room and followed petals that were plastered to the concrete walk by the rains. "Officer Debano, come with me. Let's see where this goes."

The manager stayed behind to keep people out of the room.

The detective followed Eli.

"One is here on the steps, Bwana, but they end here." Eli turned on the flashlight on his cell phone and scanned the shadowed area. "Here, they went down this path toward the parking lot."

"Keep following the trail, Deckland." Officer Debano spoke as he saw the evidence.

When they reached the far end of the parking lot, Eli stopped. "They must have put her into a vehicle here. There are no more petals." He directed his light to the tire tracks and took some photos.

"Deckland, there have been many cars and vans parked here today." The detective squatted down and looked over the area.

Eli enlarged to the photo of the tire track and showed it to the detective. "But they have smaller tires with narrow tread. These are wide tires like you find on SUVs. And this cut in this print is just like the tracks I found by the destroyed fence at my church. It's evidence. It is Aga Kahn's SUV. He kidnapped Olivia Stone."

The detective radioed his chief as he started walking back to the scene of the crime. "Olivia Stone has been kidnapped. There is strong evidence that Aga Kahn is involved. We must move fast. Her life is in danger."

Eli motioned that he wanted to speak to the chief. Debano gave him the cell phone.

"Hello, this is Eli Deckland. I'm the one who called Detective William Debano about this case. He has been investigating Aga Kahn since my wife was murdered, my church property was vandalized, and Olivia Stone was threatened by Kahn." He listened. "Thank you. I will come to the police station with him when we are finished here."

After returning the phone, Eli watched the men dust for prints in Olivia's room. Once they finished, Eli gathered Olivia's personal items and put them in her suitcase. He put her purse, phone, camera, and iPad into a plastic laundry bag and carried it with him.

He waited with the resort manager on the sidewalk until the police had finished their work. Debano left for the police station.

"Kamau, do you have a large safe in your office or at the front desk that I can put her valuables in until she returns?" Eli asked.

"Yes. In a few minutes, when the police leave the parking area, we can secure her belongings. I'll have her room cleaned so she can rest when this ordeal is over."

"Let's do that, then I'm going to the police station to make sure everything is being done to find her." *Time is critical. Minutes matter...Olivia matters.*

*****

Particles of dust danced in the beams of sunlight when Olivia woke from a night of fitful sleep. She hopped to the restroom and back, her swollen ankles seeping blood from the cuts caused by the wire-threaded rope around them. She searched for tools, for anything she could use to cut herself free, to no avail. *I can't run, can't escape. No one knows I'm missing! Lord, help me!* Panic gripped her, knowing her captors could return at any time.

She lay on the bed again and held her ankles together to relieve the pain. Swelling hampered her efforts and increased her anguish. Praying for a miracle was her only hope. She wept and cried out to the Lord to help her. *My dad needs me to come home. He's sick, Lord. Ellie and Jocelyn are counting on me. And Eli, Lord. He could be hurt or killed if he goes up against Aga Kahn on his own. I need you, Lord. Please help me!*

*****

Eli barged into the police station and walked to the investigator's desk. "Detective Debano, do you know where Aga Kahn could have gone?"

"I am gathering info, Eli. Give me a minute." He worked at his computer and wrote something on a pad of paper.

Eli paced the small office, impatient for information. The walls were a dirty gray color that clashed with the dark-green linoleum covering the floors. A row of tan plastic chairs lined one wall. Bars covered the windows that desperately needed to be cleaned. A slow-moving fan hung overhead, stirring the mixture of stifling heat and body odor.

Debano stood. "I've got the address of several places he could be holding her. You can ride with me. Some officers will follow us to each location. Let's keep looking for the black SUV he uses."

"Where are we going first?" Eli was on Debano's heels.

"To his home in Stone Town." They got into his car and maneuvered through the narrow streets to his residence. He led the way to the ornately carved door and knocked.

A meek worker answered. "Yes, can I help you?" He spoke in Swahili.

"We are looking for Aga Kahn. Is he here?" Debano slid his foot into the doorway to prevent it from being closed in their faces.

"No. He's not here."

"When did he leave? Was it early this morning?" the detective pressed him.

"He left last night after dinner and has not returned. He owns many properties in Zanzibar."

"Did he say when he will return?" Officer Debano ran his finger behind his tie. His suit and tie spoke of his detective status. His badge caught a glint of sunshine when he moved his coat to put his hand in his pocket.

"He does not inform me unless he needs a meal prepared. He usually has a meeting with his men on Tuesday mornings. He will be at his office at this hour."

The officer thanked him and turned to leave. He told the other officers to continue to follow his vehicle.

"Doesn't he have an office in Stone Town?" Eli was getting antsy.

"Yes. He's a very wealthy man who owns many properties. Some of them are registered under the name of his company. Let's check this office first, but I'm doubting he would keep Ms. Stone there unless she's drugged to keep her silent."

When they stopped in front of the building, the door was padlocked, with no vehicles parked in front.

"He's not here. Let's not waste time." He talked into his radio, giving the other car their next destination.

Eli checked his watch. It was nearly eleven o'clock. *We could be too late. Lord, protect her and give us wisdom.*

"We're leaving Stone Town?" Eli watched the ocean waves lapping the shore.

"When I researched Aga Kahn's company, I found an address. Actually, it's a plot number of a home, a mansion, really, just out of Stone Town that he also uses as an office." The detective hurried through roundabouts, going as fast as the morning chaos would allow.

"It seems logical that he would get her out of town to hide his actions." Eli ran his hand through his hair. "I just hope we're not too late."

"I'm thinking he wouldn't do anything criminal in front of his complete team of employees. He'd wait until he had given their assignments and dismissed them before he finished his plans for Olivia Stone."

"I hope you're right. I pray you're right."

Debano commanded attention as he spoke to the men following them on his radio. When they slowed to enter the lavish property, Eli counted nine vehicles in the circle drive. Aga Kahn's black SUV was parked by the front door. Asim, his driver, was waiting in the front seat of the luxury vehicle.

"Deckland, let me do the talking. Understand? He'll be angered by your presence, and we want to get enough evidence to put him away for good this time."

"I understand." Eli followed Debano to the front door. He paused by the SUV and took a photo of the nick in the front-right tire, proving his theory.

The detective opened the front door, not waiting to be introduced. They walked in on Aga Kahn's meeting, where he was addressing his staff. Anger was immediately evident on his face.

"May I ask the meaning of this rude intrusion? I am addressing my employees. We have much business to discuss." Kahn slammed his hand onto the podium in front of him.

"I warned you, Kahn. Olivia Stone has been kidnapped. After your threats toward her, your assault of her at her hotel, we thought we would begin looking for her here on your property."

"This is not my home, and those events were misunderstandings. I thought she was someone else." He crossed his arms over his chest.

"This beachfront property is owned by your company, giving you complete access at all hours, day or night." Detective Debano seemed to enjoy sparring with him.

"Do you have a search warrant?" Kahn's furrowed brow and intense gaze showed his anger.

"Not yet. But we will within the hour. Do you have something to hide?"

"No, and my men can vouch for my innocence. I do have a meeting to conclude, and they have schedules to meet. You are wasting my time. Please see yourself out the same door you entered." Aga Kahn turned his back on Eli and the officers.

Eli followed the detective through the marble-floored foyer out the front door. Debano stopped by the driver's window of Kahn's SUV. "Asim, you do a fine job driving for Aga Kahn." He talked with the driver but motioned for Eli to go to the back of the truck. "I'd like to get an upgrade like this. Does this SUV have automatic windows and doors?"

"Yes, it does." He showed the officer the buttons to push. "The mirrors are adjusted by these buttons on the door panel."

"Does it unlock when you push a button on the key fob?"

"Yes." He held up the black fob on the key chain. "I push this one button and it locks or unlocks the doors."

"What does this button do?" Debano pushed the button, and the back door rose.

Eli took that opportunity to look inside and found a petal. He took a picture of it with his phone, then grabbed it.

"Oh, Bwana. We must close it now. I will be in bad trouble." He grabbed the fob and pushed the button. "You go now."

"Thanks for the information on the SUV." The detective moved to the back of the SUV, where Eli stood.

Eli opened his hand, showing him the petal he found in the vehicle.

He motioned for Eli to follow him back to the car and the waiting policemen. He reached for his cell and made a call. "Hello, this is Debano. Can you locate the property that belongs to Aga Kahn on the beach of Kiwani Bay? We need an aerial view or a blueprint of the property immediately. Hurry. A woman's life is at stake." He closed his phone.

"I hope you have a plan." Eli waited.

"Where are those flower petals?" The investigator held out his hand.

Eli put them in the detective's palm.

He turned to an officer. "Bag these as evidence." He faced Eli. "Deckland, did you take a picture of where you found these, by any chance?"

"Yes. I'll send you the pictures now." He took his phone out of his back pocket.

"Ever thought about being a detective? You're a great investigator."

"No, but I've watched enough police shows to know that how you gather and document evidence is critical to the case." He sent him the pictures. "You have a plan percolating in that head of yours, Detective?"

"I will as soon as I get—"

His phone dinged with a message. He held up his finger as if to say, "Wait a minute." He used his thumb and forefinger to enlarge an image, then typed something into his phone before ending the call.

"There is a pool in the back, a small building that probably houses the pool pump, and there's a pool house. It is on the right side of the house toward the back. I'm betting they're keeping Ms. Stone there."

"Let's go see." Eli started to go in that direction.

"Wait."

Debano's command stopped him.

"Why?" Eli pivoted and stalled.

"I'm getting a verbal search warrant with a printed copy being rushed to this location. I have to wait for that, or our evidence will be thrown out of court. We need to do this by the book. No slipups." He stood his ground. "Wait, Deckland."

Eli was chomping at the bit, as they say in Texas.

One of the police officers spoke to Debano in Swahili. "We are outnumbered."

"I've requested backup. They are on their way."

Maybe he does know what he's doing.

CHAPTER 9

Chirping birds and ocean waves were all she could hear. No traffic noises since early in the morning, when a few car doors slammed, but thankfully no Ali Baba giving orders to put her to death. *Yet.*

Hunger pangs had Olivia's stomach growling, but that wasn't her focus. Escaping, running, and going home were her priorities. Her burning ankles had her attention. Bending the wiry rope back and forth in an attempt to break her bonds hadn't worked. She hopped to the sink and wet a rag to ease the burn momentarily. Returning to the bed, she elevated her feet to reduce the swelling. *Maybe this will help. Who am I kidding? Only a miracle will save me now.* She laid her head on the pillow and let her tears roll into her hair unabated.

*****

"The meeting is breaking up. Some of them will leave. Let's move our vehicles down the road so they won't notice we're still here." Detective Debano and Eli got in the detective's car and moved out of sight. Their police escort followed suit.

"There's another one of Kahn's men that needs to be included in this group. His name is Usama. I didn't see him in the mansion. By the witness's testimony, he's the one who stabbed Joy and left her at my gate, bleeding."

Debano added this info to his notebook. "We will find him."

"When Aga Kahn is in custody, he will try to leave the island. You better watch the port."

"He won't be free for long, Deckland. I'll send my men to pick him up."

Waiting was torturous for Eli. Assuming Kahn and his closest employees were still in the main house helped him to breathe a little easier as minutes slid by at a snail's pace.

With their backup arriving, the officers listened to the detective's instructions and moved their cars in the driveway, blocking Aga Kahn's SUV. Debano checked his cell phone. He looked at Eli and shook his head no.

"Listen, guys, there should only be three men in the house, Aga Kahn and his two right-hand men. We will arrest them, put them in handcuffs, and then in your police cars, then search every room and closet in this mansion. Ms. Stone could be drugged to keep her quiet." He checked his phone for the search warrant. "I've got it! Move in."

"You've got to be kidding me!" Aga Kahn raged. "William Debano, you will be out of a job within twenty-four hours. You've messed with me one time too many."

"Aga Kahn, you're under arrest. We can do this the easy way or the hard way, and I would hate to get blood on those white robes." Debano stepped toward Kahn, grabbed one wrist, and slapped a handcuff on it.

Aga Kahn yanked his arm away, not giving up easily.

Two officers drew their guns, trained on Kahn.

"It's over, Kahn. You're surrounded." He reached for his other arm and jerked it behind him.

His officers apprehended Kahn's cohorts and escorted them out to their police cars.

"You don't understand the extent of my far-reaching power. You're invading my territory at your own risk." Aga Kahn fumed as he was escorted out of his mansion. He was like a boxer hemmed against the ropes, with his kingdom crumbling around his feet. "You're making a big mistake. When I'm released, I will settle this score. I am innocent. There is no proof of involvement in criminal activities on my part." His voice was muffled when Debano pushed his head down, forcing him into the police car, and slammed the door.

"Detective, she's not anywhere on the main level of the house."

"Thanks, Officer Kijana. Have your men search the upstairs." He turned to Deckland. "Eli, there's a pool house around the right side of the mansion toward the beach. They're probably holding her there. Guys, Deckland and I will check out the pool house. Officer Warari, inform headquarters we've arrested Aga Kahn and two of his men. The rest of you spread out, searching the grounds. Kiambu, take Kahn's driver in for questioning. Take good notes. I think he's innocent but should know details of wrongdoing by the others and will want to clear his name. His knowledge should prove valuable when this goes to trial."

Eli followed the detective toward the pool house. It was hard not to run, to yell Olivia's name, but Aga Kahn could have men guarding her who have orders to kill her if she tries to escape.

Once they passed the side of the house, they entered an amazing garden of blooms and butterflies. They followed a sidewalk on quiet feet.

"Stop," Eli whispered to the officer. "Flower petals. Do you see them? She left us a trail."

"Clever woman."

They eased through the garden.

"There's a yacht docked at the pier behind the mansion. Its engines just fired up. They must have seen some of my men searching the grounds. They're taking off. Probably hired by Kahn to dispose of her body." Debano talked in hushed tones.

They walked gingerly down the winding path until they came to the pool. The water glistened in the noonday sun as chlorine seasoned the air. Eli found the pool house and pointed to the right, showing the detective its location.

The officer put his finger to his lips, indicating for him to keep quiet until he could assess her situation. He eased to the window but could only see part of her on the bed. Her legs moved.

He whispered to Eli. "She's alive. I can see her legs moving. I'm going to another vantage point to get a better look. We have to make sure she's alone before we let her know we're here." He moved to another window around the side of the small building.

Eli waited. Seconds dragged by like slugs on concrete.

Detective Debano stuck his head around the building and gave him a thumbs-up and a big smile.

Eli hurried to the window. "Olivia, I'm here. You're safe."

She started crying—no, sobbing. "Oh, Eli. I can't believe you're here. I didn't think I'd ever see you again. Do they have Ali Baba in custody?" She stood and hopped to the window.

"Your ankles are bound?" He reached in and touched her fingers.

"Yes. But that doesn't matter. You're here."

Her eyes were swollen, her hair a mess, and tears were making streaks down her dirty cheeks, but she looked gorgeous. "I'm so glad to see you."

Her fingers made prints on the dusty louvered window. "You gonna get me out of here so I can hug your neck?"

"I'm sure Detective Debano is getting the key from Kahn as we speak. He'll bring it and set you free. Kidnapping you will seal the deal on Aga Kahn's fate. He'll spend the rest of his miserable life behind bars or until they hang him for Joy's murder."

"You have your answers, your closure, Eli." She put her hair behind her ear.

"Yes, thanks to you. I'm sorry this fiasco caused you anguish and pain. You had to be scared to death."

"More frightened than I've ever been. I prayed and prayed, and you found me."

"I can't take all the credit. The police helped. I just followed your flower-petal trail."

"From the parking lot to the pool house?"

"No, from your room at the resort to where they put you in the SUV. They probably fell out of your pocket when they grabbed your clothes. There was one last petal in the back of the truck you were transported in."

"So you have proof he kidnapped me?"

"Yes. It's over, Olivia. You're safe. So can you stop scaring me now?" He reached through the window and wiped her tears. She leaned toward his hand.

"My hero."

*****

"You ready to get out of there? I think I hear someone coming." He smiled.

"Absolutely!"

One of the extra officers came with a key and unlocked the door. He saw her bound ankles. "I will return with some tools." He turned and hurried to his vehicle.

Eli stepped into the pool house and took Olivia into his arms. She wept as he held her. Eli kissed her hair as she cried. "It's finally over. He can't hurt you anymore."

"They were going to kill me, Eli."

"I know. A yacht was waiting at the dock, but it's gone now."

She looked up at him. "He was going to feed my body to the sharks. You got here just in time."

Eli could hear the officer returning. He held Olivia away from him and wiped her face. "Sit on the bed again so we can get your ankles free."

"Take pictures first. They forced a gag into my mouth, cutting my upper lip in two places. My wrists are bruised. The ropes are on the floor. But the ropes around my ankles have cut my skin. And it hurts."

Eli used his phone to gather evidence, then knelt to help the officer.

"The rope has wire in it. The bigger guy tied my ankles and made sure I couldn't escape." Olivia spoke as they used wire cutters to set her free. "Oh, thank you."

"Be still. I need to clean this wound." Eli got a clean towel from the restroom and wet it. "This may burn. There are dirt particles and some of the rope in the cuts." He worked on her wounds with tender hands.

"Thanks, Eli."

"Do you want to change into your clothes before the detective questions you?"

"Yes, please." She walked slowly to where they had dropped her clothes and changed in the restroom.

Debano entered and looked around the room. It needed cleaning but was a luxurious pool house decorated in an island theme. The pricey paintings on the wall had spiderwebs between them. The linens on the king-size bed were imported. He took photos and collected evidence.

Eli repeated what Olivia had told him, explaining the ropes and the gag. "She's changing her clothes. She needs a doctor. Her ankles are sliced up by the wire in the ropes they used. Is there one at the resort?"

"We'll call the manager and have one meet us there when we take her back."

"I'm going to get her a bottle of water." Eli hurried to the police car.

Olivia came from the restroom with her pajamas rolled into a ball. "Do you need these?" She held her PJs out to the police. "I don't want them anymore."

"Yes, we will check them for evidence. I am so sorry for what you've been through, Ms. Stone. Aga Kahn and his men are in custody. They will not present any further threat to you."

"I'm glad to hear that." She sat in the chair where her clothes had been. "I thought I was going to die here." Tears streaked her face again.

"I know this is difficult, but can you tell me what you remember?"

"Sure. As I was drifting off to sleep, I thought I heard something in my room, but it thundered loud and I assumed the winds had blown the shutters or something. Then I felt a presence in the room. I froze and listened, then a cloth with a sweet smell was being held over my mouth by a firm hand. It was probably the bigger guy that's always with Aga Kahn. Everything went black."

Eli stepped into the pool house and offered her a bottle of water.

"Thanks." She took a drink.

"Go slow. Take a little at a time." Eli warned.

She did as he suggested. "I woke up in the back of the SUV. I kept my eyes shut and listened to their plans to put me here and deal with me after their meeting today. I pretended to be asleep when the bigger guy threw me over his shoulder, grunting as he carried my weight through the garden path to this place. I felt something, opened my eyes a little, and saw flowers, grabbed them, and dropped petals... and you know the rest."

"Did you hear their names?"

"Fahad and Zubair and, of course, Ali Baba." She forced a small smile.

"Ali Baba?" Debano asked.

"That's what she named Aga Kahn when she met him on the port."

"Deckland, did you take photos?"

"Yes, and I sent them to your phone while you talked with Olivia. Can we get her to the resort soon?"

"They should be finished in the house. You can walk her to my vehicle while I wrap things up. Let's get her to the resort. I'll call the manager and have a physician meet us there." The Zanzibari detective left them in the pool house.

"Are you ready to get out of here?" Eli held his hand out to help her up.

She stood. "In a minute." She hugged him. "Thank you again, Eli."

He stared in her beautiful eyes. "You're very welcome."

She kissed his cheek. "I'm ready now." She took his hand and left the room of her nightmare.

*****

Eli helped her into the front passenger seat, being careful with her legs.

"I'm good, Eli. Is this your seat?"

He smiled. "I'll ride in the back on the way to Stone Town. There's more legroom up here for you."

"Who discovered I was missing?"

He sighed, then faced her. "I couldn't wait to see you and wanted to finish our conversation from last night. That seems like a long time ago after the day we've had. I went to the resort to eat with you. I waited, but you didn't come. Knowing you love their breakfast, I got concerned and went to the front desk and asked for someone to bring a key and go with me to check on you. The manager volunteered. When we got there, your door was open."

"I'm shocked they didn't shut it. But they were probably in a hurry. What about my purse, passport, and iPad?" she asked.

"They were in your room. I put them and your camera into the main safe at the front office."

She smiled and slipped her hand into his.

"I knew you wouldn't leave your passport, so the manager called security and the police. I was in a panic. I know firsthand what Aga Kahn can do, and I didn't want to lose you too. I sat down while they looked for clues. Then I saw the petals, the ones you were touching at dinner. I followed the trail that ended at the parking lot, where tire tracks of Kahn's SUV began. I knew he had you."

"I'm sorry, Eli. You've been through a lot."

"My struggle doesn't compare to what you've just experienced. I'm thanking the Lord you're okay." He kissed her hand.

Detective Debano walked toward the vehicle. "You should go into law enforcement. You're pretty good at this, Deckland."

"Oh, I don't think so. Too much work. Hey, don't forget about Usama. When he hears that Aga Kahn's in custody, he'll run. You better watch the airport and ferry."

"I've sent two of my men to pick him up." He made a phone call and got into the vehicle. "Let's get Ms. Stone to the resort. A physician will be there."

Olivia loved watching the ocean waves in the distance as they returned to Stone Town. "I don't know what to say. I knew my time was running out. They were going to feed me to the sharks. Then…you two rescued me. *Thanks* seems like such a small word."

"You're welcome, Ms. Stone. I'm glad you are okay. When are you scheduled to return to Nairobi?"

"Day after tomorrow. I'll catch the ferry that departs at noon."

"We need to debrief you, but we have some work to do at the police station first. I have some criminals to interrogate. Could I get your statement later today? Maybe around four? It will take about an hour."

"That will be fine. There is a large balcony attached to my room. You and Eli can come there. I'll have tea prepared for us."

They slowed to turn into the resort parking lot.

"I'm glad to see this place again." The corner of her mouth turned up with a small smile.

Eli reached forward and squeezed her shoulder. She grabbed his hand and held on.

"Welcome back, Ms. Stone." The manager opened her car door.

"Thank you, Bwana. I'm glad to be back."

"We are so sorry for what has happened while you were with us at Dream of Zanzibar. I have marked your bill paid in full. A physician is waiting to attend to your wounds."

"Thank you, Bwana."

The staff applauded her return when she walked through the lobby. Olivia waved as tears gathered in her eyes. Her senses were on high alert. Hearing the waves. Smelling the salty air. Watching the palms dance in the breeze. She was glad to be alive.

*****

Eli spoke to the detective, requesting that his SUV be brought to the resort for him. Then he caught up with Olivia. "Hey, I'm going to order some lunch. What do you want?" He grabbed her hand.

"Anything. You choose. I want a Coke with ice now and another with my meal. A cold bottle of water would be good too. Thanks." She squeezed his hand before releasing it.

"Sure. I'll have it delivered to your room." He hurried to the bar and placed an order, then passed the manager as he left the lobby area.

Kamau stopped Eli. "Please let me know if she needs anything. Did they catch the ones who did this to her?"

"Yes, they did. She's no longer in danger."

"That is good news." He clapped his hands and smiled.

When Eli reached her room, the doctor was looking at her wounds. He put medicine on the cuts on her lip, then on her wrists.

"Let's get you on the bed so I can attend to your ankles."

Eli hurried forward and fluffed some pillows behind her and put a clean towel over a pillow he used to elevate her feet. "You have a flashlight, Liv?"

"In my suitcase, near the bottom."

Eli retrieved it and held it on her ankles while the physician worked.

"Dada, there are some pieces of wire and twine deep in your wounds. They must come out now to keep it from getting infected." The doctor was gentle yet thorough.

"Do what you have to do. I'll be fine. Don't worry about hurting me. I have a high pain tolerance."

The doctor worked, Olivia flinched a couple of times, and Eli held her hand and the light. After about thirty minutes, he poured peroxide into her wounds, blotted them, repeated the process, then wrapped her ankles.

"Take this antibiotic twice a day until they are gone. I will leave the peroxide. Pour it over your ankles after you shower for the next two days, until the wounds close. You will recover nicely." He packed up his instruments, stood to leave, then turned back to Olivia. "I am glad you survived this attack. I'll take my leave now."

Eli stepped forward and reached for his billfold. "What do we owe you?"

He held up his hand. "The resort has covered my bill. Do not concern yourself."

"Thank you." Eli returned to Olivia's bedside and pulled a small table close. "They are delivering your drinks. The food will be here soon." He looked at her. Tears were streaming down her face. He wrapped her in an embrace and held her as he motioned for the waiter to put the drinks on the table. The waiter complied and used a bottle opener to open Olivia's drinks, then left quietly.

Eli kissed her hair. "Lord, I thank You for sparing Olivia's life today. I ask You to give her an amazing peace until the storm subsides. Give her sweet sleep tonight. Do not let the enemy steal another moment from her. We are so thankful for Your hedge of protection, Your guidance, and Your strength through this trial. We are forever grateful. Amen."

He kept her in his embrace and started singing. "Amazing grace, how sweet the sound that saved a wretch like me. I once was lost, but now I'm found. I was blind, but now I see."

Olivia faced Eli. "That was perfect."

He took a napkin from the table and wiped her cheeks. "You thirsty?"

"Parched."

He opened the bottle of water and gave it to her. "Drink slowly."

She looked around the room at several beautiful flower arrangements. "So many beautiful flowers. Who sent them?"

"I think the resort did that. I would have, but I've been busy." He took the bottle of water from her and poured some Coke. "Try a sip. It's really cold. Our lunch should be here any minute." He watched her.

"Don't look so worried. I'm going to be fine. I just had to have a good cry."

He put a strand of hair behind her ear. "You sure?"

"After your prayer, I'm sure."

A waiter knocked on the open door.

"Put it right here, Bwana."

The waiter arranged their food on the table, then removed the stainless steel covers that were keeping their entrees warm. "Anything else, Bwana?"

Eli took some shillings out of his pocket and offered them to the young man. "The manager is tipping me for this delivery. Asante, Bwana."

As he left, Eli pocketed the money and served Olivia her lunch. "You hungry?"

"I'm starving."

Eli prayed over their food before he took a bite.

"You haven't eaten either, have you?"

"Nope. There was a damsel in distress, and she needed a hero."

Olivia smiled. "The Lord used you today, Missionary Deckland. You saved me, and I'm glad you have the closure you needed concerning Joy's death."

"You did that for me, Olivia. I appreciate your diligence, even though it almost cost you your life." He caught a tear sliding down her cheek.

"I think that's why I came to Zanzibar, to help you. You're free to move to the next chapter of your life with your precious Judah."

"Trust me, I've been praying a lot about what's next. I don't have all the answers, but I have a special peace that it will be good."

They ate in silence, with the sounds of ocean waves serenading them.

"You said you came back to talk with me this morning. What were you going to say?" She held her fork, holding her next bite.

"You've been through a lot today. After you finish eating, why don't you rest until I return with the detective? May I join you for dinner tonight?"

"I'd like that." She put her hand on his.

"I'll get your things out of the safe while you finish your lunch. You might want to check your e-mail, since your dad's been so sick. I'll have someone bring your belongings to you. See you at four." He kissed her hand, then brushed a soft kiss across her lips, careful against her wounds.

"Thanks, Eli. You think of everything."

"I try." He winked and left.

Olivia turned and watched him go, admiring his profile and the confidence in his stride, a fine male specimen. She pivoted and took a bite of juicy pineapple and enjoyed the seascape in front of her through the wall of windows, memorizing it. Her eyes filled with tears when she thought about leaving on the ferry. *I'll leave my heart on this island when I walk away.*

CHAPTER 10

Debano met Eli at the entrance of the police headquarters. "Deckland, I'm serious about you considering law enforcement. We could use your skills. You've wrapped up this case for me. Have you considered my offer?"

Eli laughed. "No, I can't say that I have. I'm called to influence lives so there are more people following God's laws and less breaking man's laws."

"Well, man, I owe you on this one." He motioned for him to his office.

"I do have one request that could call it even." Eli stepped into the crowded space, where files were stacked on the messy desk and a landline rang from a buried phone.

"What's that?" Debano shuffled some papers and pressed a button on the phone.

"I want to see Aga Kahn behind bars. It would do my heart good and close a tough chapter for me." He paused. "Can you make that happen?"

Debano met his gaze. "It is against regulations, but I'll appeal to the judge." He punched a number into his cell phone and spoke in Swahili.

Eli sat in a plastic chair in front of the desk and waited.

"Well, that's a first." He looked at Eli. "He said yes." He grabbed his keys. "Come on, I'll drive you."

Eli followed him to the potholed parking lot.

Debano cranked the car and pulled into the chaos of a traffic jam.

"I guess you'll leave the island soon."

"That's the plan. It's time to start a new chapter."

"Well, Zanzibar is blessed that you've lived on our island. I know it was at a great cost to you, but Christianity can now spread without fierce opposition."

"Then my mission is complete and Joy's life has made a difference." Eli took a deep breath and released it slowly as that truth sank into his heart.

*****

"Move. I will sit there." Aga Kahn barked orders in the dusty jail cell.

"Yes, Aga Kahn." Fahad stood and gave Kahn the only chair in the crowded space.

Clang clang clang. The guard banged a mallet against the bars. "The ground is level here. You are no longer in authority, Kahn. Stand and give him the chair, or I will remove it and the cots."

Kahn ignored his directive.

"Now! Stand up, Kahn. You've lost your throne."

Kahn's gaze sent daggers toward the jailer. He stood and motioned for Fahad to take the seat. Fahad hesitated.

"You must." Aga Kahn's demeanor had diminished a bit. "I insist."

Fahad took a seat but kept his eyes on his leader.

The jailer moved on to other cells.

"I'm sorry, Aga Kahn. I would never disrespect you in this way," Fahad whispered. "When we are released, I will pledge my loyalty to you again."

"You have not failed me, Fahad. You have been a faithful employee."

"Kahn, step to the bars. You have a visitor!" the jailer yelled from down the hall. "Grab the bars."

Kahn bent toward Fahad. "Maybe our release has been arranged. They fear my far-reaching power and influence." He moved to the bars as a light blinked. When his eyes adjusted to the flash of light, he knew he was wrong. "You!"

"Yes, it's me, Aga Kahn." Eli took another photo of his angry face. "It relieves me to see you behind bars. Your evil ways have finally caught up with you."

"Deckland, leave. You have no right to be here. Jailer! Get him out of here!" Aga Kahn demanded.

"Kahn, your royal reign is over. Lower your voice." The jailer stood firm.

Eli stepped close to the bars. "Aga Kahn, I don't delight in your incarceration, but you must pay for your crimes. Your man Usama has been apprehended, and he confessed to killing my wife, as you directed him to. Your fate is sealed. My prayer is that you accept Jesus as your Savior before they hang you."

Kahn banged on the bars, then reached through, trying to strangle Eli. "I will never renounce Allah!"

Eli stepped out of his reach. "Goodbye, Aga Kahn." He turned and left the jail area, allowing the door to slam behind him, proclaiming the end of the threat.

*****

"Place the tray on the balcony, please, Bwana." Olivia led the way and opened the door.

"Anything else, Ms. Stone?" He paused.

"Yes, I'd love a plate of fruit."

He started for the door. "I will return with your fruit."

When he opened the door, Detective Debano and Eli were there.

"Asante, Bwana. Come in, guys. He just delivered tea and coffee." She led the way to the balcony and took a seat facing the ocean. "Feel free to fix your drink to your liking." She poured hot water over a tea bag in her cup and added sugar. She got comfortable in a canvas captain's chair and propped her feet into an extra chair.

"How are the ankles, Olivia?" Eli leaned close and lifted the loose bandage.

"They're sore, but they'll heal in a few days." She stirred her tea. "I'm taking in this beautiful seascape and counting my blessings."

Eli squeezed her shoulder and took the chair beside her. "Are you ready to answer the detective's questions?" He poured coffee into a cup.

"Yes, after you assure me Aga Kahn is in jail."

"Relax. He will never touch you again. He's in custody." He reached for his phone and pulled up a photo. "Look at this." He held his phone for Olivia to see her kidnapper behind bars, with his men in the background.

She smiled. "That makes me happy. Send me that picture."

The detective put his cup on the side table. "Ms. Stone, I have listed your complaints against Aga Kahn as stalking, attempted murder, and kidnapping. Is that correct?"

"Yes. Will these charges be added to the attempts on Judah's life and the attack on Eli's church and the loss of his wife?"

"They will be addressed in the charges that Deckland is filing. Can you tell me what happened last night one more time? I want to check my notes for any detail I've missed."

Olivia started the story with thunder in the distance and ended with hearing his and Eli's footsteps outside the pool house and thinking she was about to be murdered.

"Was it Aga Kahn giving instructions to the other two men when you reached the seaside property?"

"Yes."

"Who carried you?"

"The bigger one, named Zubair. The guy named Fahad unlocked the door and helped tie me up and gag me."

"Did you have any dealings with this guy?" He showed her a photo of another Indian man, Usama.

"No, I've never seen him."

The waiter from the restaurant delivered Olivia's fruit.

"Bwana, I will sign this to my room." Olivia put her hand out for a pen to sign the ticket.

"Ms. Stone, our manager, Kamau, instructed me that it is a gift to you."

"Please thank him for me." She smiled at the young man.

He bowed. "I will."

"Sorry for the interruption, Detective."

"Do you have anything else to say about your kidnapping, Ms. Stone?"

"Only that I'm thankful you two found me in time."

"I think you have Eli to thank. He discovered your disappearance and followed the flower petals until we found you. He was a man on a mission."

"He is a missionary, Detective," Olivia said.

"But this time you were the mission." He stood. "I think I have what I need. If you will sign these three documents, I'll take my leave."

Eli looked at the papers. "These are your formal complaints against Kahn."

She signed the papers, then poured herself another cup of tea while Eli walked the officer out.

When he returned, he leaned over and kissed Olivia. He kept his face close to hers. "I'm so sorry for what you've been through. It had to be a horrible experience." He kissed her forehead and took a seat after putting his chair closer to hers.

"You look tired. Is it hard work being a hero?" She put her cup on the table.

He laughed. "Oh, I think you're the brave one." He reached over and took her hand.

"I'm all out of courage for today." She turned so she could see his expressions. "But I'm peaceful it's over."

He paused, staring at the ocean waves hitting the shore. "There is another part of this tragedy that I didn't realize until today. By stopping Kahn, you vindicated Joy's death, but it also cleared the way for Christianity to spread freely across the island. Her death and your bad experiences have great spiritual implications. You made a difference, Olivia. I hope that fact will help you heal."

"I'm glad, Eli. What Joy wanted to accomplish will now be done. Mission accomplished for the Deckland family."

"I haven't thought about it that way. But it's satisfying now that I'm leaving this mission post."

Olivia yawned.

"You're tired. How about you rest a bit? Can I still have dinner here with you tonight?"

"Yes, see you at seven o'clock."

"I will meet you in the restaurant." Leaning over, he gently kissed her lips, then stepped into her room, pulled a red rose from a bouquet, and took it to her on the balcony. "Some petals for you, Olivia."

"Thank you." She took the rose and lifted it to her nose.

Eli slipped out of her room.

*****

Olivia chose a tank top with a light jacket to go with long pants to hide her bandaged ankles. After applying a touch of color on her wounded lips, she donned flashy jewelry to draw attention from her eyes, which seemed to tear on their own. She checked her reflection once more before strolling on polished rock sidewalks toward the restaurant. Her palms grew sweaty as she got closer to Eli.

The employees applauded when she stepped into the reception area.

She smiled at them. "Thank you, so much."

Kamau stepped forward. "Good evening, Ms. Stone. We are very happy you are safe. May I walk you to your table?"

"Yes, please." She followed him, taking in the tropical setting with slow-moving fans moving above them, candlelight adding ambiance to the lush Zanzibari decor.

Eli stood when Olivia reached the table. "You look lovely."

"Thanks."

The manager left them as Eli pulled out her chair. "You okay?"

She put her napkin on her lap. "I will be. I'm feeling so many conflicting emotions." She teared up.

"It will take time. You survived a near-death experience. It's understandable." He motioned for their waiter and ordered a Coke for her. "Let's enjoy our time together. Maybe I can get your mind off the past and as we focus on the future." He winked at her.

The waiter delivered her soda.

She took a sip. "That's good." She put her glass on the table. "And how are you going to do that?"

"By telling you stories about Judah."

"That will work."

"He has asked about you. I'm truthful with him, but I don't think he understands." He looked down, then met her gaze.

"Is he sleeping better?"

He nodded. "He is. Seeing you has helped him."

"I'm glad. He's special to me." As tears threatened, she moved to stand. "I'm hungry. Let's visit the buffet."

"Lead the way."

While enjoying beef shish kabobs and grilled vegetables, Eli told Judah stories. "He was born in Dar es Salaam during the rainy season. We got stuck axle-deep in slick black cotton soil, trying to reach the ferry to get back to Zanzibar. I carried Joy and Judah from the taxi to a dolla dolla, one of those trucks that carry people on benches in the back of the vehicle under a canvas cover. Judah slept through it all. We were soaked by the time we boarded the ferry, but so happy to have our baby boy."

"And he is a treasure, that's for sure. Did you two want more children, Eli?"

He put his fork down and stared at her. "We hadn't talked about it. Judah was so small when she was murdered." He watched her reaction.

She looked down at her plate, then at him again. "This beef is so good. I think I'll get more." She stood and joined the buffet line. She'd changed the subject to keep her tears at bay. *Whatsoever things are pure, whatsoever things are lovely... think on those things.* She'd reminded herself of those words all day, but it was hard to keep her focus when so much was warring with her thoughts.

She returned to the table. "They just brought out some flan. You want flan tonight?"

"Sure, I'll get us some." He stood.

She caught his hand and whispered, "Get us three servings."

He laughed. "You're pretty popular around here. I don't think they'll mind if you have an extra dessert."

"I'll order us some tea."

"Great."

He served her two flans and took his seat. "We have one more evening together. Would you join me for dinner on the dhow? I have reservations for us at seven."

"Sounds wonderful."

"You sure you're up for it?"

"I wouldn't miss it. I'll rest in and pack tomorrow, then watch the waves under the swaying palms as long as I can."

He looked around. "This is a gorgeous resort. I hope your good memories of Zanzibar outweigh the bad."

"Oh, they do, and I have the pictures to prove it. Could you send me some pics of Judah? Mine were blurry."

"Sure." He did it on his phone as she watched the wind blowing that stubborn curl that fell on his forehead. High tide raised the volume of the crashing waves. Nocturnal noises filled the air. Olivia memorized the moment.

Eli looked up. "I sent several." He sat back in his chair and studied Olivia's face. "I thought I was going to lose you today, Liv." He sat forward, moved their dessert plates, and took both of her hands in his. "This morning I wanted to tell you that I cherish you, Liv. You've made me feel things I've never felt before. I want 'us' more than anything. Will you give this relationship a chance?" He waited.

She smiled. "Eli, you've broken down all the walls I'd built around my heart. I care about you, so much." She paused. "I don't see how our lives and our careers can blend, and you know I feel inadequate. You deserve so much more. But I will pray about it."

He smiled. "Then I will talk to the man upstairs and lean His decision my direction."

"That's not fair, Eli. Missionary prayers rank much higher than mine."

"That's not true. He listens to your every whisper. He loves you, Olivia. He rescued you today for a purpose. I want to be part of the future He has planned for you." He kissed her hand.

"You have a way with words, Eli."

"I mean every word." He stood and helped her with her chair. "May I walk you to your room, or would you rather I kiss you good-night right here in the restaurant?"

She smiled. "Well, since you put it like that, you can accompany me to my room."

The moonlight highlighted the tips of the waves as they strolled the grounds of the resort. Eli put his arm around her shoulder, keeping their connection until they reached her room.

"I'm glad you joined me for dinner." Olivia put her hands around his neck and pulled him toward her for a kiss. "You're quite a man, Eli Deckland."

"I'm glad you think so, Ms. Stone." He kissed her again. "Enjoy your day tomorrow. I'll pick you up at six thirty."

"And I'll be waiting."

*****

Eli parked his SUV and pocketed the keys. The wood-carver's market was one of his favorite places in Zanzibar.

"Habari, Bwana. Hello, sir. Are you going to spend the afternoon with us today? We are working hard."

"I would love to watch you work, Willie, but I must hurry today. I have an appointment later. But I will come back another day." Eli hurried through the market, kicking wood shavings and sawdust as he walked. "Paul." He lifted his hand in a wave.

"Hello, Bwana Eli. I have some chess sets for you to see. Come and sit." He wiped sawdust off a slice of a log and sat on its end for a stool.

"Thank you. I know this is a rush order, but my friend is leaving the island tomorrow."

Paul opened one chess set wrapped in newspaper and handed it to Eli.

"Paul, this is great work. I love the wood grain of the pieces. Do you have a larger one?" Eli gave it back to him.

"Yes, Bwana." He put the smaller chess set aside and reached for a much larger package. Smiling. A larger one meant more shillings. Being careful not to scratch the wood, he cut the tape holding the newspaper wrapping. He gave it to Eli.

"This is a beautiful chess set. Paul, you do such good work. He'll love this. It's perfect." He ran his hand across the smooth wood-grained surface.

The wood-carver smiled and began rewrapping the set.

"How many shillings, Paul?"

He kept wrapping.

"Paul?"

He stood and stepped close to Eli and spoke in a whisper. "Do you have American money, Bwana? My daughter is going to the US for a trip, and she needs their kind of money."

"Yes, Paul. I can pay you in dollars. I don't carry it with me. I can return with the dollars tomorrow afternoon. Just tell me how much to bring. I'm glad to help you."

He shook his head and smiled. "That would be a great blessing."

They made their deal, and Eli left with the chess set for Olivia. Other wood-carvers attempted to sell him more carvings, but he was sniper-focused on getting to the other side of town, to Olivia.

*****

It took a while for Wi-Fi to connect. When it did, Olivia quickly sent Jocelyn a message.

> J,
>
> I am keeping my original schedule. I will meet you and Ellie at the hotel in Nairobi. I have a lot to tell you both.
>
> See you soon,
> Liv

She pressed Send and sighed, deep in thought. Mixed emotions played tug-of-war with her heart as she packed her bags. Sudden sounds made her jumpy.

Dressing for the evening proved challenging. Bruises on her neck, wounds on her wrists and ankles had to be camouflaged. Donning a long gauzy sundress and bejeweled flip-flops, her favorite hoop earrings, and a matching clip holding her hair in an alluring updo, she readied for her last date with Eli. Eye shadow and extra mascara might keep his focus off her injuries and on her face. The carved bangle bracelet she'd purchased for her aunt perfected her look. After applying coral-colored lip gloss, she grabbed her handbag, checked the area outside her door, then strolled to the lobby to wait.

Who would have thought a handsome missionary would claim her heart with such finesse? He played his cards right and staked his claim. *But is this a good idea? It works in my heart, but I can't make it work in my head. Lord, give me wisdom.*

*****

Eli was standing by his SUV, trying to look casual as she approached.

"Is that your *GQ* pose?" She lifted her phone and caught the picture. "You're a handsome man, Deckland."

"Ms. Stone, you're definitely model material in that outfit with your alluring eyes glowing in the moonlight."

"I bet you say that to all the girls."

He laughed and kissed her cheek before opening the door for her. He hurried around the truck and slid into the driver's side. "Only you, Ms. Stone." He cranked the vehicle and plunged them into traffic. "Did you rest today?"

"Yes, and packed my luggage. I tried to pack all my emotions, but they kept escaping before I could get the suitcase shut." She gave him a small smile.

"Does it feel good to be safe?" He glanced at her as he navigated a round-a-bout.

She put her hand on his on the gearshift. "Yes, it does, but it may take a while before eerie shadows, loud noises, or sudden movement don't make me jump." She glanced at his profile. "You went above and beyond to save me."

He smirked. "I did call in a few reinforcements."

"Oh, so the police force works for you now?" She grinned.

He laughed.

She loved the sound. "You're different."

"A huge load has been lifted. But let's not replay the terrifying parts of your visit. Let's focus on us." He pulled into a parking lot, exited the truck, and opened her door.

"Sounds like a plan."

"But before we board the dhow, I have something for you." Eli reached back into his vehicle and grabbed a bottle of water and put it in her hand.

"What's this for?"

"Your less-drowsy Dramamine." He took a package out of his pocket and opened it.

She took the tablet and handed the remaining tablets to him.

He pushed her hand back. "You'll need them tomorrow. Keep it."

She dropped them into her seat of his SUV. "Thanks, Eli."

He took her hand, shut the door, manned the locks, and pocketed the keys. "You're welcome."

They walked toward the dock, where a small crowd waited for the gangplank to be lowered. The area was framed by swaying palm trees and a variety of boats tied off on a series of piers. It was a nautical parking lot.

"How old is this pirate ship?"

He put a strand of hair that had escaped her clip behind her ear. "I'm not sure. There are two that work the island and others that work up and down the coast. I'm sure the tour guide's spiel will fill us in. The menu for tonight is steak and prawns."

"Smells great from here. I love the fragrance of grilled meat."

She focused on him. He wore a long-sleeved dress shirt with the sleeves folded to his forearms, highlighting his bronze tan. His dress pants were classic. He carried himself like royalty, offering his heart on a silver platter. It was a struggle not to fall into his arms and declare her love.

"What?" He questioned the look on her face.

She gave a small shake of her head.

"Are you memorizing again?"

"Yes." *Before I say goodbye.* Her heart ached.

CHAPTER 11

"A table for two, candlelight, soft music, and wonderful food, on the Indian Ocean—you've outdone yourself, Eli." Olivia pivoted, taking in the setting.

"I'm glad you approve. I wanted to make a memory that would carry you until we see each other again." Eli pulled her chair out.

"About that…" Olivia wanted to share her heart.

"Let's wait until the dinner cruise is over to talk about where we go from here. I want to memorize our moments." He kissed her hand.

"Are you making fun of me?" She smiled.

"No, but I want to savor my time with you." Eli motioned to the waiter, who delivered a bouquet. "For you, Olivia." He presented her with a mixed bouquet.

"They're beautiful. What kind of flowers are they?" She smelled the blooms.

"They're flowers that grow on the island. The scarlet ones are found on the flame trees, these pink and purple ones are called bleeding heart, this green foliage is called the eternity plant, the coral ones are called coral butterfly, and this colorful plant is called Zanzibar croton. I thought you deserved them after all you've experienced in Zanzibar."

She leaned over and hugged him, leaving a kiss on his cheek. "You're pretty amazing."

"I'm glad you think so."

"And you kiss good too."

He laughed.

After the captain welcomed his passengers, Olivia could tell they had left the dock by the rocking of the ship on the open water. Donning his Captain Hook costume, he told the history of the dhow and the adventures that had been witnessed by the pirate ship.

The Tanzanian band on board provided live entertainment in Swahili and broken British English. The clanging lead guitar covered most of the mistakes that the keyboard player made, but they were trying hard. Their loud singing camouflaged most of the musical mayhem.

A waiter in steampunk attire served their soup and drinks and soon followed it with steak and prawns that were prepared perfectly. "We decorated your plate with colorful vegetables. I hope you enjoy your meal."

Olivia cut one of the prawns and savored the taste. "This is such wonderful food."

"I'm enjoying this steak myself." He took another bite.

"Do you cook, Eli?"

"No, but I can man a grill with the best of them."

"Eli, tell me about your family." She tried the vegetables that decorated her plate.

He took a drink of water. "My parents are successful realtors who work side by side but still have a strong marriage. I'm the eldest of three. My brother, Justin, is enjoying a career in the Navy, and my sister, Patricia, is a pediatric nurse. She's in a serious relationship with a lawyer named Aaron. We're just one big happy family."

"Have any of them traveled to Africa?" She popped another prawn into her mouth.

"Mom and Dad met us in Kenya for a safari before we started language school to learn Swahili. They loved it. Any more questions?"

She put her fork down and watched his expressions. "Tell me about Joy's family. Does Judah have grandparents, aunts, and uncles in his life?"

He hesitated. His fork clanged as it hit his plate. "Yes, he has grandparents that adore him. They live in Austin, Texas. Joy had two sisters, Carolyn and Janet. Both of them are married and live outside of Houston. Judah has three cousins close to his age."

"I'm sorry if that's hard to talk about."

He rubbed the back of his neck. "It's okay. I just hadn't given that part of a future between us much thought."

The waiters chose that moment to enter the dining area with trays of desserts raised above their shoulders. In a choreographed move, they turned and lowered the trays at each table and allowed the diners to make their selection.

Tea and coffee were served with flair.

"They have worked hard to make this experience memorable."

When she finished the last bite of her dessert, he leaned forward and kissed her lips. When he drew back, he put his fingers on her lips. "Let's walk around the ship. Looking at Zanzibar from this vantage point is spectacular, and the full moon makes the top of the waves look like diamonds."

She stood.

He placed his hand at the small of her back, guiding her to the east side of the dhow.

"Wow, it's beyond magnificent. It does look like diamonds spread out on black velvet."

"The ocean puts on this display when we have a full moon." He put his arm around her and drew her close. "Your arms are chilled." He rubbed up and down her arms quickly, trying to warm them, then embraced her.

She leaned back and gazed into his amber eyes. "I'm going to miss you, Eli. I've grown accustomed to your presence in my life. It's been acerbated by the battles we've faced. But your strength and integrity and your ruggedly good looks have captivated me, overriding the challenges. But...I need time. I see in you everything I've ever wanted in a man, but have the exotic tropical setting, the adrenaline rush of adventure, and the smile on Judah's face clouded the future possibilities of 'us'?" She put her fingers on his lips to keep him from interrupting her diatribe.

"You carry a heavy-missions call on your life that I don't share. You're lonely and possibly still grieving the loss of a faithful wife. I can't have the additional children you'll want one day. Can we make a rational decision after just two weeks together? I know the facts hit hard, but we have to examine it from all angles." She moved her fingers to his cheek, loving the masculine scent the wind swept her direction.

He put his hands on both sides of her face and paused. "I think I'm in love with you, Olivia. From the first moment I touched you, I've been drawn to you, addicted. I've never felt this way before. I understand the complexities of our relationship, but we don't run from challenges. We face them head-on, and that's what we're going to do. I don't have our answers, but I'm not going to let you go. Give 'us' a chance. That's all I ask." He sealed it with a passionate kiss.

Still in his embrace, Olivia whispered, "I want to, Eli. I really do."

He kissed her once more.

She felt so safe in his embrace. "I think we're almost back at the pier. I hate for this evening to be over."

"I'm glad you enjoyed it." He led her back to their table to retrieve her flowers. Then they followed the other diners to the parking lot.

After they were in his SUV, he leaned over and kissed her again before starting the truck. "How about having some hot tea poolside at your resort?"

"Sounds great." She replayed his words as he maneuvered the vehicle through the bumpy streets of Stone Town.

*****

While stirring sugar into his tea, Eli considered her concerns. "I heard everything you said, Olivia, and it sounds like you've thought long and hard about this." He motioned from himself to her, meaning "me and you."

"When you've been kidnapped and think your life could end, you think about unfinished business, like being there for my father, my friendship with Jocelyn and Ellie, and you, Eli. You're so special to me." She looked down, then met his gaze. "I hate to leave you."

He kissed her hand. "We will walk through that door tomorrow."

"Yes, we will."

"Are your suitcases full?"

"Almost. Why do you ask?" Olivia had questions on her face.

"I have an amazing chess set in the back of my SUV for your dad."

"You remembered. I'm excited. How heavy is it?"

"I don't break a sweat when I carry it. But I'm concerned about making your luggage overweight."

"I'm a flight attendant. I don't have to worry about that."

"Perks of the job again?"

"You guessed it." She smiled.

"I'll get it out for you when you're ready to go to your room."

"How much did it cost?"

"Why don't I collect the money when I see you in the States?"

"You're a missionary resorting to blackmail?"

"Whatever works." He laughed.

*****

Still reeling from Eli's final good-night kiss, Olivia slipped off her shoes and lay across the bed in her room. She pulled a flower out of her bouquet and felt its petals as she thought about the man who'd stolen her heart.

Her cell chimed with a message from her dad. She sat up and called him. He answered on the first ring.

"Hello, Dad. Are you okay?" She waited.

"Yes, everything is fine. My infection is gone. I have two more days of antibiotics. I sent a text to tell you my surgery is scheduled for the tenth at 8:00 a.m."

"I'll be home on the eight. I'll come over as soon as I land."

"No, Olivia. You'll be in jet lag. Go home take a good shower, get some sleep, then come by the next morning for breakfast. You'll be wide awake then."

"That sounds like a good plan. But, Dad…"

"Yes."

"Are you okay? I mean, really okay?"

"The doctor says I'm stabilized and I'm strong enough to do well with the surgery."

"I'm glad. I'll walk through this with you. You're going to be fine."

"I needed to hear you say that."

"I leave Zanzibar tomorrow, then fly from Dar Es Salaam to Nairobi, where I'll catch my working flight home. I've arranged to take emergency leave to be with you for two weeks after we get you home. Aunt Jana Rose will feed us and make sure you regain your strength."

"But she'll boss me around. She's always been a getter-done person, but I love her cooking, so let her come if you have to."

Olivia laughed. "You love your sister, Dad, and she'll be with us every step."

"I think I'll take a lot of naps since I'll be too weak to torment her." He laughed.

"At least you haven't lost your sense of humor."

"See you in a few days, Liv."

"Bye, Dad."

*****

Eli tossed and turned all night. He tried to pray, but it seemed like his prayers were hitting the ceiling. Dreading Olivia's departure had his thoughts in desperate mode. He had to find a way to keep her in his life. *Lord, I need some help here.*

As the sun lightened the horizon to a peachy haze, he took a long shower, then dressed for the day. He kissed Judah on his head but kept his distance to keep from wearing his breakfast.

"Frances, I'll be here for dinner tonight." He grabbed his keys.

"Sawa, sawa, Bwana. Okay. Judah will be glad." She looked at Eli and paused. "You okay?"

"I'm taking Ms. Stone to meet the ferry after breakfast."

"I'm sorry, Bwana. That has made your heart sad. I can see it." She gave Judah a piece of toast with jelly. "Share the words of your heart while she is with you. She will hear them over and over in her thoughts."

"Good advice, Frances. I'll do that. Hey, if you need to bring Becca here into the main house while Jessicah rests, it is okay."

He ruffled Judah's hair before he left the secure compound, rushing to eat up the kilometers. He arrived at her resort an hour early for breakfast.

"I'm having breakfast with Ms. Stone. I will wait at her table and enjoy some of your amazing coffee."

"Follow me, Bwana." The manager picked up two sets of silverware wrapped in linen napkins and led the way to Olivia's assigned table.

"I appreciate your kindnesses to Ms. Stone after her difficult ordeal."

"We are very thankful you found her in time to save her life. Enjoy your breakfast. It is complimentary, or on the house, as you say in the States."

"Thank you. I appreciate that."

He turned over Eli's coffee cup. "I'll get you that coffee."

*****

Olivia planned to sleep in, but praying and wishing and hoping only allowed a couple of hours of slumber. Her impending departure tied her stomach in knots. She argued both lines of thinking, the pros and the cons of pursuing a relationship with Eli, not unlike two lawyers battling in court. But neither side won. The stalemate would have thrown their future together out of court. Tears stained her pillowcase when she planned what she would say to Eli. *I love him. What do I do about that?*

Giving up on going back to sleep, she dressed for her trip to the mainland and closed her luggage, then went for an early breakfast. When she reached the reception desk, she requested for someone to retrieve her luggage and gave the manager her room key.

"I will take care of it right away. I'm glad you stayed with us, Ms. Stone. Please visit us again if you're ever in Zanzibar."

"I will do that, Bwana."

"Ms. Stone, there is a distinguished gentleman having coffee at your table."

She smiled. "Then I better get over there." She turned and saw Eli staring at the beach while he stirred his coffee.

She approached quietly. "Is this seat taken?"

He stood and hugged her. "You're early."

"I couldn't sleep." She laid the remains of her bouquet on the table, took a seat, and turned her coffee cup over, signaling for it to be filled by her waiter. "I had a lot on my mind."

He reached for her hand across the table and twined his fingers with hers. "I know what you mean. I was restless myself. But an early breakfast gives us extra time together. Let's visit the buffet."

Olivia ordered her eggs over easy. Eli ordered an omelet. They selected an array of fresh fruit and bread before meeting back at their table.

"Their food is delicious. Pray over our food so we can dig in." Olivia put her linen napkin on her lap.

Eli took her hand and prayed for their food and guidance and peace as they said their goodbyes.

Olivia had tears in her eyes when she raised her head. She leaned back so they could place her plate of eggs and crispy bacon in front of her and used her napkin to wipe under her eyes.

"I talked to my dad last night. He called as I was getting ready for bed." She took a bite of her eggs.

"Is his infection gone?"

"Yes. His chest is clear, and his surgery is scheduled for two days after I get home." She held her bacon in midair.

"I'm glad. I bet he's ready to have you in the States."

"He seems to need me to be there. This hasn't happened since we lost my mother." Enjoying her crispy bite, she buttered a piece of toast.

"You've just taken two weeks off to visit Zanzibar. Can you take off the time to be with your father and not have an issue with your job?"

"I've been a workaholic and haven't taken any time off the last two years. I have a month of vacation days that I can utilize. When I told them about my dad's surgery, they approved the time off. No problem." She dipped her toast in the orange marmalade.

"I'm glad."

They ate their meal, making small talk about Judah, the missionaries coming to replace Eli, and Olivia's best friends meeting her in Nairobi.

"What will you do after I leave?" Olivia asked.

"Besides being sad and racking my brain for ways to make this long-distance relationship work, I've ordered lumber to begin building the crates I'll use to ship our personal belongings to Texas. I'll meet with the deacons of my church and begin the transition to my successor. And I may have to testify against Aga Kahn in front of Parliament. There are a lot of details to be completed when you leave a mission post, and a lot of paperwork is required. Beyond that, I'll be busy missing you."

"That was a mouthful." She smiled and sat forward with her elbows on the table. "I'll work my way home, then see my dad through his surgery until he's healthy again. Then I'll go back to work. I came to Zanzibar considering making a change, to make a difference somehow. But I didn't find a place for me here on the island." She looked down, pulled a petal off one of the remaining flowers in the bouquet he'd given her, then looked at Eli. "Life will go back to normal, with one exception: I'll be missing you." Her eyes filled with tears. "Eli…"

He squeezed her hand. "Olivia, you're a ravishing woman who stepped into my life at the perfect moment. You've captured my heart." He kissed her hand. "We can do this. I know we can."

"Your love is speaking louder than my concerns. You make me believe it's possible."

"It is possible." Eli put his heart out there.

She smiled.

He leaned back. "I'd love to sit here with you all day, but we need to get you to the port." He stood and helped her with her chair.

She bade the staff goodbye and got into Eli's SUV while he loaded her luggage.

"You're carrying the chessboard?"

"Yeah. They'll let me put it in a compartment during flight. I wrapped the pieces with my clothes. He's going to love it. It's perfect." She slid into the front seat.

He got behind the wheel, leaned over, and kissed her.

"Thank you for saving my life, Eli."

"I did it so you would spend it with me." He winked, then cranked the vehicle.

"There's always a catch." She smiled.

He got them through Stone Town and headed toward the dock without incident.

"Are you in a hurry to get me to the port?" She looked at his profile.

"No. I just want to get you there safely without us getting stuck in a traffic jam." He paused as he downshifted the vehicle. "If I had a choice, I'd keep you here."

At the port, he was able to park near the bulkhead so they could watch the activity until the ferry arrived. He held up a bottle of water. "Did you take your Dramamine?"

"Not yet." She dug it out of her purse and took it with his water. "Thanks."

"The ferry's coming." He looked toward the water.

"I know. Let's sit here until all the passengers have disembarked." She reached for his hand.

"I hate this." Eli pulled her into his arms.

"I do too." Her tears dampened his shirt. She kissed his neck, then pulled back, wiping her face.

"That beautiful smile is struggling through your tears." He caught a tear with his thumb.

"I'm trying not to ugly-cry in front of you." She wiped her face with the back of her hand.

He attempted a smile. "It's time to go. People are boarding. Kiss me one more time."

She leaned close and kissed him. "Bye, Eli." She touched his lips.

He got out and went to the back for her luggage. She tore some petals off one of the last three flowers and dropped them in his seat before opening her door.

He pulled her luggage toward her and hugged her for a long moment, kissing her hair. When she stepped back, he dropped a small card into her purse. "E-mail me when you're home safe. Let's keep connected as often as we can. Okay?"

"Okay." She hugged him again. "Bye, Eli." She kissed his cheek, then pulled her luggage toward the gangplank, dropping petals every few steps. After giving the captain her ticket, she boarded the ferry and moved to the rail and turned back toward the shore, toward Eli. Tears streamed down her face unabated. She waved goodbye, then pulled out a flower and dropped a petal overboard. As the ferry left the port, she dropped another petal. He gave her a thumbs-up. She dropped petals until he could no longer see her, then threw the stems overboard. *I hate goodbyes.*

*****

It hurt to lose Joy, but seeing Olivia leave ripped his heart in two. Breathing was hard. He bent over and closed his eyes to catch his breath. It was déjà vu. When he opened his eyes, he saw flower petals blowing toward his feet. *Olivia, I got your message loud and clear.* He picked up a couple of petals, dusted the sand off, and watched the ferry until it vanished in the distance.

When he opened the door of his SUV, he spied the petals she left in his seat. He picked them up and slipped into the seat. He wiped his tears before he cranked the vehicle, but couldn't move yet. Saying goodbye was rough, but going forward would be arduous at best. He grabbed his water bottle and guzzled the water Olivia had left. After taking a few deep breaths, he put the truck in gear and pulled into traffic. Getting his work done, finishing the adoption process for Becca, and preparing his church for a change of leadership stood in the way of his departure. He hurried around a traffic jam, anxious to get started, anxious to fly the African skies again. His destination: Olivia Stone.

CHAPTER 12

Olivia wept until she couldn't see Eli anymore. She hiccupped, blew her nose, then turned to look for a place to sit. Making her way to an empty bench, she parked her luggage beside her and sighed.

"Would you like a bottle of water? I have two, and water helps when you're upset." An English-speaking African woman handed her a bottle.

"Thank you. Goodbyes have never been easy for me." Olivia opened the bottle and took a long drink.

"Goodbyes reveal how we feel about somewhere or someone. It is then we can know our hearts." She patted Olivia's arm. "Listen to what your heart is saying."

"Are you a counselor or something?"

"Yes. I work in Dar es Salaam. I was in Zanzibar for holiday."

"By *holiday* you mean a vacation, don't you?" Olivia asked.

"Yes. It's a great place to visit."

Olivia smiled, remembering Eli saying that phrase. She drank more water as the shore of Tanzania came into view.

She held on as the ferry bumped against the pilings, Olivia thanked the woman for the water and pulled her suitcase toward the queue of those ready to leave the ferry. Seeing taxies lined on the shore, she was anxious to see Jocelyn and Ellie, ready to get back to America. She retrieved Eli's card from her purse. It was a normal business card with his information on one side. On the other side of the card, he'd written, "Miss you already." She held the card to her chest as tears flooded her eyes again.

When the vessel was tied off, Olivia hurried to a taxi. "To the airport, Bwana."

"Nyerere International?"

"Yes, Bwana. I'm catching a flight to Nairobi."

He loaded her luggage and started the meter before plunging them into a traffic jam of cars trying to leave the port.

Olivia hung on for the rough ride. It reminded her of the bumpy trip she endured in Aga Kahn's SUV, especially as she saw men wearing long robes and turbans in Dar es Salaam. Goose bumps dimpled her skin. She reminded herself Kahn was in prison, but the nightmare kept popping up. It was time to go home.

*****

Judah loved running around the yard while Eli built two shipping crates. The pieces of lumber he cut off made great blocks for his chubby little hands. Hammering the crate allowed Eli to work off his built-up emotions as he watched the shipping crates take shape. Manual labor was therapeutic to his aching heart. He missed Olivia with a vengeance.

Frances kept an eye on the boy as she fed Becca a bottle, rocking her in the porch swing.

"Frances, I'm going to assemble the crates on the front porch so we can pack them for shipment. The height of the porch would make loading the crates easier. Let's start with Joy's things. I'll wrap my curios and carvings that will fill the crate."

"Yes, Bwana. Let me know when you're ready for me to pack more boxes." She put Becca on her shoulder to burp her.

"As soon as I'm given the date when the new missionaries are arriving, we'll pack more boxes and start on our suitcases. We will move to a guesthouse while I sell the furniture, unless the new missionaries want to buy my things. I'll e-mail them and ask. It could save me a lot of work and get us off the island a few days sooner."

Frances smiled. "I think Ms. Olivia has something to do with your haste."

"Yes, she does." Eli returned her smile.

"Does she know about Becca?"

Eli paused. "I didn't mention Becca because I wasn't sure I'd be allowed to adopt her. How is Jessicah today?"

"It won't be long now, Bwana. She is getting too weak to be up for more than a few minutes. She isn't strong enough to hold Becca's weight anymore. It is sad."

"Yes, it is. I'm glad I took some photos of Jessicah and Becca together before she got so sick. I'll show Becca the pictures and tell her about her mother."

"Like you do for Judah?"

"Yes. Two sad stories."

"But I think there will be one good ending if you play right."

"You mean if I play my cards right. I plan to do that, Frances. I will let you know how our story ends." He smiled.

"Please do. Bwana, would you watch Judah for me while I put Becca in her bed?"

"Sure, I can." Eli gathered more pieces of wood and added to Judah's pile, bringing applause from his dirty little hands. He taught him how to stack the blocks into a tower and push them over. Laughter bubbled out every time they did it. When Judah went inside for a snack, Eli put his blocks into a box, saving them for future playtimes.

Finishing the crates ticked off one item on Eli's list. He moved Joy's boxes into the crate, stacking them tightly for shipment. He closed it and draped plastic over the wooden shipping box. Pausing to remember her, he spoke into the wind. "Joy, you didn't die in vain. Bringing Aga Kahn to justice for ordering your death lifted the barriers that fought our message. Now, Christianity can spread across Zanzibar unobstructed. Many will come to know the Lord because of your bold witness and great sacrifice. You completed your mission. Well done, Joy. You made a difference."

Closure on Joy's part of his life felt complete. Finally.

Eli put his tools away and spent the evening with Judah. His energy and laughter were medicine to his soul. Judah trusted Eli to catch him when he stumbled. Squatting down put Eli eye to eye with his son. "Judah, the Lord says to come to Him as a child. The way you trust me, I will trust Him with our future with Becca and Olivia."

Judah clapped his hands and said, "Yay!"

Eli knew his son had no idea what he'd said but loved hearing his voice, just like the Lord heard us when we prayed.

*****

Aga Kahn was livid. His robe was dirty, and the food was subpar.

"Bwana, I need to speak with you." He stood at the bars, waiting for a response.

"You have to wait, Kahn. We are getting another prisoner. I think he's a friend of yours."

Aga Kahn walked a few paces to the right and stood in the sunshine that beamed in from a solitary high window.

Watching for birds to perch on the windowsill or fly by on their way to the port. Each day the whistle of the approaching ferry caused him to wonder if the Decklands had finally made their departure.

Hearing footsteps, he turned to see Usama, his employee, being put into their overly crowded cell.

"There is no room for another prisoner, Bwana. Put him in another cell."

"I think you've forgotten something, Kahn." He unlocked the door and pushed Usama forward. "You're no longer in power, so I don't obey your commands." He slammed the door and locked it. "Now, sit down and keep quiet." He took a step, then turned back. "If you men decide to kill one another, don't make a mess."

The jailer turned and left the prisoners in a stare-down with Usama, whose failure to complete Kahn's directives had led to the return of the Sahar of Zanzibar, which got them into their current situation.

"We meet again, Usama." Aga Kahn stood, towering over the man. "What do you have to say for yourself?"

Fahad stood beside Kahn. "What have you told the police about our work, Usama?"

"I told them the truth. The work was completed, proving our power and your authority, Aga Kahn."

"But with us being in custody, Christianity can spread at will!" Fahad shouted and lunged at Usama.

Kahn raised his hand, stopping Fahad's attack. "Usama, did you tell them I ordered you to kill Joy Deckland?"

"Of course, Aga Kahn. They know who you are and how you've worked to keep Islam strong on the island. They will release you soon. Of that I am sure."

Fahad tried to get to Usama again. "We are being charged with murder, attempted murder, and kidnapping.

Including Aga Kahn. And you have given them the information they needed to end us. All of us."

Usama crumbled to the floor. "No!"

Aga Kahn paced the cell, planning Usama's demise. As his sandals crunched sand on the dirty floor, he racked his brain for a way out of this grave situation.

Fahad put their one chair close to the window and stood on the seat so he could watch freedom from the cell. The freedom they had lost.

*****

Olivia hurried to the hotel, anxious to see her friends. When Ellie opened the door, Olivia fell into her arms and wept.

"What's wrong, Liv?" Jocelyn rushed toward Olivia, pulled her luggage and a large square package in, and shut the door.

Ellie walked her to the bed and grabbed a tissue for her from the dresser.

Olivia hugged Jocelyn. "I'm glad to see you both."

"Why the tears? Your wrists are bruised, and your lip is cut. Why are your ankles wrapped? What happened in Zanzibar?" Ellie sat on the bed while Jocelyn took a chair that faced Olivia. They waited.

Olivia blew her nose and took a deep breath. "I was stalked, attacked, and kidnapped. A handsome missionary rescued me. I fell in love with him and just had to say goodbye. You know I hate goodbyes." She started sobbing again.

Ellie spoke over her sobs. "Hold the phone! You were attacked and kidnapped. What's that about?"

"Give me a minute." She got up, used the restroom, and washed her face. She propped herself up on one of the beds with several pillows and started from the beginning. "I got seasick on the ferry on my way to Zanzibar…"

Ellie and Jocelyn listened, asking questions from time to time.

"I left a trail of flower petals from his truck, over the gangplank, and floating on the water."

"Asking him to follow you, to find you," Ellie finished her story.

Jocelyn sat forward in her chair. "So you're getting over a traumatic experience, you haven't slept, you haven't eaten, and your heart is broken."

Tears wet Olivia's cheeks as she nodded. "Yes."

"Does he love you, Olivia?" Ellie asked.

"Yes, but he will see that it won't work. I'm not a missionary, I can't give him more children, and our occupations won't mesh."

"How did you leave it with him?" Jocelyn moved closer to Olivia.

She pulled out his business card. "He gave me this and asked me to e-mail him when I reached the States."

Jocelyn took the card, read it, turned it over. "Already missing you." She put the card in Olivia's hand. "That's special, Liv."

"And he is truly amazing." She took out her cell phone and showed them his picture.

"Wow! He's hot, Olivia. I don't get it. What's the problem? You've proved you'll travel and you're willing to live anywhere. You love Jesus, and you love him." Ellie got animated. "All that's left is a 'happily ever after.'"

"But he's going to want more children that I can't give him. I'm not…" She couldn't say the word.

"Nonsense! You're perfect for him. You're strong, adventurous, and drop-dead gorgeous. Any other talents, you can learn," Jocelyn said.

"All but one. Motherhood."

Ellie hugged her. "It's going to be okay. We're together, and we will talk this out and find a solution, Liv. And if we can't figure it out, we will pray! So we've got this covered."

"We missed you, Liv." Jocelyn squeezed her hand.

She blew her nose. "I think you're going to miss me again. My dad had a heart attack, and they've scheduled his open-heart surgery two days after we get home. I'm taking at least two weeks off to be with him. He said he needs me. I'm praying we will be close again like we were before we lost Mom."

"The Lord will be with you. Jocelyn and I will be praying the whole time," Ellie said.

Jocelyn stood. "I vote we have dinner and go to bed early. Things always look better after you sleep on it. Then tomorrow, let's see the sites and do a little shopping before we have to work the late flight home."

"Dinner sounds great. I'm starved!"

*****

Eli packed a few boxes of books just as the sun lightened the sky. He taped and labeled the cardboard boxes and stacked them by the wall of his bedroom. After a shower and a shave, he dressed in a pair of khakis and a sports jacket. He needed to visit a faithful member of his church in the hospital. If his condition didn't improve, he would be transferred to a hospital in Dar es Salaam for surgery.

"Da-Da."

"Morning, Judah. Good morning, Frances." He poured himself a cup of coffee and served his own breakfast.

"Judah, eat your eggs." Eli forked a small serving and put it in his mouth.

He signed thank-you.

"You're welcome."

Eli ate a piece of toast with orange marmalade and finished his coffee. "I have a busy day with several meetings. I'll see you two at dinner tonight."

He kissed Judah, grabbed his keys and briefcase, then left for Stone Town. He visited the man from his church who seemed to be improving and wouldn't need surgery.

Stepping into the police station, Eli met Detective Debano. "Hello, Deckland. I was studying Joy's case earlier today. Usama's confession confirmed the details we gathered. It will close this case and bring a strong verdict."

"How is the case on the kidnapping looking?" Eli took a seat across from the detective's desk.

"All our evidence is strong. It will lead to a conviction. But one thing I wanted you to understand. If they try the case of Joy's murder first, which they probably will because it happened first, they will get a guilty verdict and sentence Kahn to be hanged, then the other cases may not be heard."

"They become a moot point if he's dead." Eli ran his fingers through his hair.

"Right. Are you okay with that, after all you and Ms. Stone have been through?"

He sighed. "As Americans, we want to have our day in court. Olivia deserves that, but if Aga Kahn is sentenced to death, it won't matter in the eyes of the court."

"That's what I'm saying. Punishment for all his crimes would be achieved at his death. I hope that you and Ms. Stone will see this as justice being served and be okay with it."

"Will I need to testify? I'm preparing to move to the States." Eli stood and walked to the door.

"I may need you to sit for a deposition. I can video your testimony. I've done that before. But this is such a high-profile case I think the judge will push it to the front of the docket."

"He could. Just let me know when you need me to show up. I have a couple of weeks left on the island. Thanks for your work on Joy's and Olivia's cases. I appreciate the way you've walked through this with me."

The detective stood and came around his desk and shook Eli's hand. "It has been painful for you, but you stood strong and didn't give up. I'm glad I could help."

Eli made his way across Stone Town to the office of Emily Mungo, the children's officer handling Becca's adoption. After waiting twenty minutes, he was escorted to her office.

"Hello, Bwana." She stood and shook his hand.

"I won't take much of your time. I was wanting to check on the Becca Mongaine adoption. Can you give me an update?" Eli sat on the edge of a leather sofa across from her desk.

"First, how is Jessicah doing?" She took her seat behind her desk.

"Not good. She isn't strong enough to pick Becca up anymore. She will pass within the next few weeks."

"What a sad story! But I'm glad Becca has a chance for a good future. I've submitted all the paperwork required and the video we made at your home. Since I've been out of the country, I had several cases to present. I put your case first in the lineup, and I'm hoping to get a positive answer, granting your adoption at any time. I will call you immediately."

"I appreciate your work on this case." He stood to leave.

"Please inform me when Jessicah passes."

"I'll do that. Good day." Eli went to his SUV and stopped in Stone Town for some of that wonderful pizza he and Olivia had enjoyed. The pizza was great, the memories haunting.

Driving through Stone Town, Eli went to the port to arrange for the shipping of his crates and stopped at a jewelry store to see if they had what he needed. He decided to save Joy's ring and give it to Judah someday when someone captured his heart. He searched for something special for the Sahar of Zanzibar; it had to be stunning for a beautiful woman, an enchanting lady.

*****

Olivia and her best friends shopped at the Massai Market in Nairobi, an open market of vendors offering their handmade items. They bought giraffe carvings, woven bags, African art, and lots of custom jewelry. Bartering was a challenge they enjoyed.

Lunch at Java House, an American-owned restaurant in the heart of the city, was a wonderful stop before they visited the giraffe park. They hand-fed the giraffe, and when Olivia put the pellets in her mouth, he took it, wiping his long slimy black tongue across her mouth.

"I got a perfect pic of the giraffe kissing you, Olivia. I'm going to frame it for our mantel." Ellie grinned and showed her the shot on the screen of her camera.

"Print me a copy too." Olivia wiped slime from her face. "Judah would think it's funny."

Jocelyn turned. "Judah?"

"Eli's adorable little boy." Olivia smiled. "I'll show you some pictures. You will love him. But we need to hurry. Our driver said we could feed some baby elephants. You game?" Olivia put her arms through their elbows, and they walked out arm in arm.

"Let's go meet Dumbo." Ellie dodged a little Kenyan boy who was wandering around.

They climbed into their rented van and arrived at the Sheldrick Elephant Orphanage in no time.

Jocelyn was reading a brochure about the orphanage. "Olivia, do you want to adopt a baby elephant? You get a monthly update via e-mail about the one you choose to adopt." She led them to a sign that explained the process.

"It supports the daily care of the pachyderms. I love that. Let's do it." Olivia headed to the main office, and they started the paperwork.

"Ladies, you can feed some of our babies and, after seeing our orphans, select the one you want to adopt, then on your way out, you can give me the name of your elephant."

"Thank you, sir. We'll do that." Jocelyn led the way to the stalls where the babies were.

They fed them their bottles, took great pictures, and after all the orphans hurried in from the field, they chose their favorite elephant.

"Help me. Liv! He won't let me go!" Ellie called out for help when Maisha, a baby elephant, wrapped his trunk around her.

Olivia and Jocelyn laughed at her dramatic antics as they took great pictures. The elephant trainer smiled as he helped release her from his grip.

She patted the elephant and posed for a picture. "That does it. I'm adopting him! Olivia, let this be a lesson to you. When a male chooses you, you don't let him get away!" Ellie dusted off her clothes as she marched to the office to make her adoption final.

"I think she's ready to go." Jocelyn started to follow her.

"Yep, her mind is made up." Olivia smiled and caught up with the spunky blonde.

"I enjoyed the giraffes, but the baby elephants were so much more fun," Ellie said as they waited to complete their adoption papers. "But you two probably enjoyed kissing the male giraffe more. But that was a little too much tongue for me."

"El, it was an eighteen-inch slash of slime! We did it for the photo op." Jocelyn wiped her cheek again. "I hope I got it all off."

"I think you did, J." Olivia checked her watch. "If we go back now, we could have a nap and a shower before dinner. It will help us work all night."

Jocelyn opened the van door and waited for them to enter. "Sounds like a plan, but I want my shower first."

*****

Eli's cell phone vibrated with an incoming call. He smiled when he saw Emily Mungo's name on the screen. "Hello, Ms. Mungo. I hope you have some news for me."

"I do. It was unanimous. Your adoption of Becca Mungaine has been approved. Stop by my office to sign some documents, then her last name will become Deckland."

"Praise the Lord! That's wonderful! Thank you for helping this be completed in such a short time."

"You're welcome, Bwana. I love happy endings. Becca will be loved and cared for under your watchful eye. Congratulations."

"See you soon."

Eli walked to the back of his house. Frances was taking Jessicah's dried clothes off a drooping clothesline. Judah played with his blocks on the back porch.

"Frances, is Jessicah awake?"

"I'm not sure." She turned and put her hand out toward the boy. "Judah, let's visit with Ms. Jessicah."

Judah joined Frances in the yard. His strawberry-blond hair was highlighted by the African sun.

Frances tapped on the door. "Jessicah, Bwana, and Judah came for a visit. Are you awake?"

"Yes. I'm watching Becca play with her toy."

Eli led the way as they stepped into her room. "Hello, Jessicah. I have great news. The adoption is final. I have to sign a document and her surname becomes Deckland."

She smiled. "Makes me happy. It's hard to say thanks." She patted her heart as a sign of her appreciation.

Eli squeezed her hand. "Becca will be safe. Rest now." He picked Judah up and took him back to their house to play as he packed a few more boxes. After dinner, Judah's bath, and bedtime, he checked his e-mail, knowing it was too soon to hear from Olivia. But he had to check before he called it a day. Exhaustion pulled him into slumber pretty quickly.

After about four hours of sleep, Eli heard his back door open, then soft footsteps grew louder as they reached his bedroom door. *Jessicah is going to heaven tonight.*

"Bwana, it is Frances. I need you to come. Jessicah is dying."

Eli was up and had his jogging pants on in a flash. "I'll be right there, Frances, after I call the doctor."

"Thanks, Bwana." She sniffled. "I will go stay with her."

Eli walked to the worker's quarters, which were directly behind his house. He entered Jessicah's room and sat in a chair beside her twin-size bed.

"Bwana…"

"Don't try to talk, Jessicah." He patted her hand. "The doctor is coming."

"Hard to breathe. I go soon…" She struggled to inhale. Frances helped her sit up a bit to catch her breath.

Jessicah touched Frances's face. "Love you."

"And I love you, Jessicah."

Jessicah turned her head toward Eli. "Love my Becca."

"Do not worry. She'll be loved and cared for. You gave her life. She will be grateful. I will tell her about you, Jessicah. I'll tell her how much you loved her."

"Asante, Bwana." A tear seeped from the corner of her eye into her hair.

"Kiss her for me…" She coughed, then exhaled for the last time.

Silence shrouded the room. Frances wept silent tears in reverence to the loss of life. Jessicah's struggle was over. Eli stared at the sweet peace on her countenance. He closed her eyes, then covered her face with her sheet.

The loud gate at the compound's entrance announced an arrival. "Frances, the doctor is at the gate. I'll tell him she is gone. He will need to see her body, then someone will come to take her to prepare her for burial."

"I will stay with her until they take her away." Frances wiped tears from her cheeks.

"Thanks. Then try to rest. Becca and Judah will both be up early. Tomorrow morning, let's talk about a small service for Jessicah."

"A service would be nice. You have been kind to her, Bwana."

"It's the least I can do." He hung his head and left the room.

Eli spoke with the physician and made preparations for her body to be removed, then climbed into bed as his clock read three thirty in the morning. *Lord, my heart is heavy and my shoulders are burdened with the responsibility of raising Becca. I'm trusting You for direction for me and my two children.*

CHAPTER 13

Tears threatened Olivia's makeup when she stood in front of the full-length mirror. "I didn't think I'd ever wear this uniform again."

Jocelyn stepped up behind her. "I think your kidnapping was more traumatic for you than you've let on. You need to talk with a counselor after your dad has his surgery, so you can heal emotionally."

"It was terrifying, Jocelyn. They were going to feed me to the sharks!"

Jocelyn hugged her. "You're safe now, and the nightmare is over."

"She's right. Let's work our way home, and we'll find a counselor for you, Liv." Ellie closed her suitcase and stood it next to Jocelyn's by the door. "You're working first class on this leg of the journey. And I don't think it's full. It will be an easy flight for you."

Olivia wiped her eyes, straightened her jacket, and faced her friends. "Let's do this."

With luggage in tow, they filed out of the hotel room, through the lobby, to their van. Upon arrival at Jomo Kenyatta International Airport, they cut in line, walked through security and down the long hall to their gate, ready to return to the African skies.

Olivia fell back into their routine with ease of greeting passengers and serving refreshments.

Jocelyn came to check on her after dinner had been served. "How are you doing?"

"Okay, I think. It feels good to be back in my normal surroundings, but I'm well aware that every air mile we travel puts me farther away from Eli, but my dad needs me."

"You're like a piece of stretched-out elastic right now. You just need some relaxation, sun, sand, and seas."

"But…that's what got me into this mess in the first place!"

Jocelyn laughed. "That and a very handsome man."

"You're not helping. You know that, right?" Olivia smiled.

"Okay, then I prescribe hospital waiting rooms, cafeteria coffee, and some long juicy e-mails traversing the miles from one certain missionary."

Olivia smiled. "That sounds like a plan."

A passenger pressed their Flight Attendant button.

Jocelyn put her hand on Olivia's arm. "Think about what you're going to say in your e-mail. The time will pass faster."

"I'll do that. Thanks, J."

*****

There was a salty breeze that cooled the heat of the noonday sun as Happy started singing Jessicah's favorite song, "God Is So Good." About twenty church members gathered at the grave site to pay their respects. Ms. Emily Mungo stood with them. Frances held Becca while Judah enjoyed running his cars in the dirt that would cover the cemetery plot.

"Thank you for coming to honor Jessicah Mongaine. Without a family of her own, she wanted to be put to rest here by her church, near her church family."

He scanned the small gathering. "Each of us has a birth date, and someday we will have a death date. The important part is what we do with our lives between those two dates. Jessicah lived well, displaying her love for the Lord at every opportunity. She loved her church and loved her baby girl. Jessicah had a servant's heart and a sweet spirit. She served us well as an employee, but she'll be remembered as a dear friend. Her life was cut short, but her love will live on in the life of her daughter, Rebecca Joy Deckland. I've gone through the process of adoption, making Becca my daughter."

Those gathered applauded, happy about the child's future.

"It is with sad hearts we lay Jessicah in this grave today, but as Christians, we have a sacred hope knowing that we will see her again. There will be a day when she will be reunited with her daughter on streets of pure gold just inside the pearly gates of heaven."

Eli prayed for those who mourned her passing. They sang songs of the church until her body was in the grave and covered with dirt. Flowers were placed at the head of the grave.

Frances took one flower and put it in Becca's little hand. She held it for a moment, then dropped it on her mother's grave. Eli got the photo to show her someday.

Becca began to fuss.

Frances turned to Eli. "I'll get the children to the truck, Bwana."

"You may have to dust Judah off before putting him in his car seat. He enjoyed the dirt pile. I'll finish here so we can get the kids home for their afternoon naps. You may need a nap too, Frances. You didn't get much sleep last night."

Becca started crying.

"I'll give Judah a snack and feed Becca her bottle."

"Sounds good." Eli greeted the children's worker, said goodbye to his church members, and made sure the men working the grave site were finished. He closed and locked the gate to the church property with the attached cemetery and looked at the pile of fresh dirt with the one lone flower near the center of the mound. It looked lonely. He took a deep breath and exhaled slowly. *Maybe that's my heart talking. The grave is next to the portion of fence Olivia financed. I miss her. Life is precious, and memories must be cherished. And I have to get to the States...to Olivia.*

*****

"New York City never looked so good." Olivia leaned toward the square window by her backward-facing seat.

"I love that view every time we come home. But after your experiences, it has to be a welcome sight," Jocelyn said.

Olivia surveyed the skyline as the Boeing 787 banked left to line the plane up for landing. All the passengers were in seat belts, with their seats in an upright position. It was that period between "all my work is done here" and "saying hundreds of goodbyes" that flight attendants enjoyed, a reprieve before facing the hubbub of the international airport.

"How long are we in New York, J?"

"Three and a half hours. Enough time to eat, relax a bit in the British Air lounge, and send a few e-mails." She smiled at Olivia.

When their wheels touched down on the runway, Olivia texted her dad that she was back in the States, then pocketed her cell to finish her work responsibilities.

Walking out with the other flight attendants was part of their routine—an expected sight in airports.

"How was your flight, Ellie? I didn't see you all night." Olivia caught up with her in front of the entourage.

"Let's just say the sardines were restless."

"I thought it was, 'The natives are restless.'" She watched Ellie's weary expression.

"Not if you're packed in like sardines for a very long night. I don't think any of them slept more than an hour. I know the babies didn't."

"Sorry. Maybe you can catch a nap before we work our next flight." Olivia reached for her bag of Kenyan curios. "Let me carry that. You look exhausted."

Being ushered to a table ahead of the line, they parked their carry-ons and ordered their food.

Olivia sent an e-mail to Eli using her iPad.

> Eli,
>
> I've made it safely to New York. I only
> have a minute, but I wanted to say...
> I miss you.
>
> Olivia

She pressed Send, then put her device away. She smiled, knowing those few words were a beginning for them.

*****

Looking through the window of the police car, Aga Kahn scanned the people entering the Parliament building for his trial.

"Fahad, my lawyer must have informed Deckland of my appearance today. He is among the crowd at the front doors."

"Aga Kahn, they could call him as a witness, and he knows too much. I was hoping he had left Zanzibar." Fahad leaned over to see who was in the gathering. "My wife is there, with her head hung in shame. It is a sad day, Aga Kahn."

"Do not fret, my friend. I still have a plan. I'm using my wealth to help us today. This is not the end for us."

"Asante, Aga Kahn."

Guards of the court approached the car and led them both to join Usama and Zubair into the courtroom. The guests in attendance hushed as the four men were ushered to their seats at a long table facing the elevated judge's desk.

Aga Kahn's lawyer came to sit with them. He spread out four folders on the table and spoke quietly to Aga Kahn. "Kahn, I'm going with a defense stating your men are so loyal if they heard you mention a desire of yours, they did those things to please you. You're only guilty of talking, and your men think they were doing a service to Allah."

He leaned toward Fahad. "Fahad, I think I can get your charges down to breaking and entering and kidnapping to preserve our Islamic beliefs. I think that will get you a small sentence."

Aga Kahn turned toward Paul Njiko, his lawyer, and spoke softly. "What of Usama and Zubair?"

"They may hang Usama for the stabbing of Joy Deckland. The main charge against Zubair is his part in the kidnapping and causing Deckland's son to be sick when he delivered tainted milk to their compound. I'm trying for a small sentence for him."

"If you make this happen, you will be greatly rewarded." Aga Kahn patted him on the back.

Paul Njiko took a piece of paper out of his briefcase. "I need you to sign this so I can receive the payment you have promised for these four trials." He gave him a pen.

Kahn signed the document as the guard who escorted them from the police car stepped forward and faced the crowd. "All rise."

Everyone stood.

"The Honorable Judge Sayo presiding."

The judge entered, wearing long black robes with a white wig.

"That's not the judge I thought we would see today. This is not good. He's a Masai, a stickler for details," the lawyer told Aga Kahn.

"You can be seated," the guard demanded.

The judge surveyed the gathering and banged his gavel on his desk three times, demanding silence. "Good afternoon, court. We are going to take the cases of these four men individually but consider them simultaneously. Their crimes overlap, which will become a web we will unweave together. We are beginning today with Aga Kahn." He looked at Kahn. "Aga Kahn, please stand for the reading of the charges against you."

Kahn and his lawyer, Njiko, stood.

The judge handed a piece of paper to the bailiff. "Please read the charges."

"Aga Kahn, you are charged with ordering the death of Joy Deckland, destroying the security wall at the Christian church, burning the Christian church, attempting to murder Olivia Stone, ordering the attempted murder of Judah Deckland, and kidnapping Olivia Stone." He looked at Kahn. "How do you plead?"

"Not guilty." Aga Kahn spoke boldly.

A murmur rose among the crowd. The judge banged his gavel. "Quiet, please."

"Opening statements will now be presented," the judge said.

Kahn's lawyer stood and gave a moving speech about the loyal followers carrying out deeds to please and find favor with the respected leader of Islam in Zanzibar. "His only crime was trying to force the Sahar of Zanzibar to leave the island because her presence posed a threat to all Muslims. He is not guilty of these crimes. The evidence will prove there is no blood on his hands."

The lawyer Hezekiah Muziki, who was hired to prove Kahn's guilt, stood. "First, let's clear up one important bit of information. Aga Kahn is a self-elevated leader on the island. He is not related to the respected Kahn leaders by blood. He's a fraud. Next, let's make it clear, if you give a command to kill someone, you are guilty of their murder under the statutes of Parliament in Zanzibar. If you order the destruction of the Christian church and its security wall, you are guilty of those crimes. If you choke a tourist until they're near death, that is attempted murder. When you send tainted milk to someone and they get typhoid, that is attempted murder. If you drug a person, carry them to an undisclosed location, bound and gag them for hours, that is kidnapping. Aga Kahn, giving orders from your pedestal of power makes you guilty of the crimes when they are carried out. The evidence will prove these charges, and we will see that justice is served and you will be punished for your many crimes." He took a seat.

*****

Eli watched Kahn squirm as Hezekiah Muziki made his powerful speech.

Detective Debano leaned toward Eli. "I think he's surprised at the strength of our case. He is getting nervous."

"This will be fun to watch." Eli got as comfortable as he could on the wooden benches.

The judge asked both lawyers to approach the bench. They talked in whispered tones, then the lawyers returned to their tables.

"Kahn's lawyer has allowed the accusing party to present their case first. Then he plans to prove his client's innocence." The judge looked at Muziki. "You can begin."

He stood and spoke for almost an hour, giving details and showing photos proving his case beyond a shadow of a doubt on every charge. There were pieces of evidence, like the photos of Olivia's neck after he hurt her and pictures of the tire tracks by the fence at the church, that surprised Kahn and his lawyer, who whispered back and forth.

"In considering the guilt of Kahn's men, they've given their detailed testimonies, saying they were acting under Aga Kahn's orders on every count. You can hear from them individually today saying the things we have presented to Your Honor in print. I also have testimony by video from Olivia Stone and Eli Deckland, if the court wants to view them. Their words reinforced the evidence I've presented today. Eli Deckland, the widower to Joy Deckland, is present in court today, if you would like to hear from him. The question is, What is your pleasure, Judge Sayo?"

"Continue."

"Your Honor, this detailed evidence proves the guilt of Aga Kahn on all charges. It also details the guilt of the other three defendants for their part in the crimes committed. We gladly present these cases for your consideration. With utmost confidence, I rest my case." Muziki bowed to the judge and was seated.

The judge checked his watch. "I declare a fifteen-minute recess before we hear the rebuttal from Aga Kahn's lawyer." He banged his gavel, stood, and left the bench.

Eli stood and stretched. "I'm going to grab a soda or some tea. I'll be back."

The detective acknowledged his departure but was in deep conversation with Muziki, who had just made a great case against Kahn.

Eli perused the kiosk just outside the building. "Great, a cold soda." The nationals preferred their sodas warm. Eli guzzled it, enjoying the fizz and the cooling effect in the tropical heat. He hurried inside, not wanting to miss any of the proceedings. The judge was on the bench, and Kahn's lawyer was beginning his rebuttal of the charges when Eli slid onto the wooden bench. The hard, rough bench reminded him of the church pews of his grandmother's church in the wild-woods of southern Georgia, uncomfortable, with a chance of splinters. He wished for one of those funeral fans.

"Judge Sayo, I'm honored to be standing before you. We've had a long list of charges presented today, but they are merely a series of misunderstandings." He turned to address his audience. "I want to begin by reminding those in attendance of Aga Kahn's prestigious position as the leader of Islam on Zanzibar Island. He deserves to be treated as such." In his practiced lawyer way, he paced as he made his points. "Aga Kahn holding Olivia Stone against a wall while instructing her to leave Zanzibar was only a display of his devotion to Islam. There is no blood on his hands, and Olivia Stone still lives. Men who love and respect Kahn have done things he mentioned, as I stated in my opening remarks, but they carry the guilt for their actions, not Aga Kahn. Kahn didn't commit any of the crimes that have been listed against him today. No photos have been presented proving his guilt. No fingerprints have placed him at the scene of the various crimes. Without proof, he is not guilty. I ask for these charges to be dismissed for insufficient evidence. We are wasting your valuable time, Your Honor."

He took his seat and was greeted by a pleased Aga Kahn.

The judge paused, as if in thought. No one moved.

"I want to view the videos of testimony that have been mentioned today. I'll be reading the statements given by Fahad, Usama, and Zubair that have been submitted, along with scanning all the photos in evidence. We will convene in two days at noon for my decision. Our prisoners will remain in custody until that time. I intend to return with a collective sentence for the accused men in custody at this time. I see this as a web of crimes that have affected too many people for too long. I assure you, justice will be served in my court." He banged his gavel. "Court is adjourned." He banged his gavel again, then stood and left.

Kahn was stunned.

The bailiff motioned for the prisoners to be escorted out. Kahn wanted to keep speaking with his lawyer but was forced to leave with his men.

Eli leaned toward Debano and Muziki. "What did he mean by 'a collective sentence'?"

Muziki smiled, leaned back, and spoke. "He sees through the haze and knows they were working under Kahn's orders. He's going to return with a verdict and sentence all four men."

"Wow. I think Kahn has met his match." Eli stood to leave. "He's going down this time."

"Yes, he is circling the drain, as you say in America." The detective smiled.

"See you in two days," Eli said as he headed home. It was time to leave Zanzibar. He had boxes to pack.

*****

Kahn jerked his arm out of the officer's. "No reason to push me. I don't like to be touched."

"Then move faster and get back in your cell, Kahn. You're just another prisoner to me." The jailer slammed the door, locked the cell, and turned to leave.

"You better hope I don't get out of here."

The officer stopped and pivoted. "What did you say? Was that a threat, Kahn?"

Kahn raised his hands in surrender. "I was talking to Usama."

"You're not fooling me, Turban. I will make a note of your threat on my report."

Kahn slammed his hand against the door, only to cringe back in pain. "I want to see my lawyer now!"

"Keep your voice down. I think he's waiting to talk to you, all four of you," the jailer said over his shoulder as he left.

Kahn paced the cell until Njiko came down the hall. "What did the judge mean by a collective sentence? It sounds like in two days' time, he is going to decide our fates without hearing the separate cases and allowing us to defend ourselves."

"That is what he said. It surprised me too. He has that privilege but hasn't exercised it in all the years he has been on the bench—that is, until today. The judge thinks the evidence we have laid out gives him the full picture of what happened and wants to study it and make a ruling."

"And four verdicts!"

"Yes, four verdicts. I requested a meeting with him to plead your case, Aga Kahn, but he declined. Unless you have additional evidence or witnesses, my hands are tied."

"Tied! Where does that leave me?"

The lawyer stepped back from the bars. "I thought we had a great defense—flawless, in fact. Except for the attack on Olivia Stone, you didn't do the crimes yourself. Your innocence was clear. I'm shocked at his decision to lump the cases together. Do you have anything to add to your defense?"

The jailer stepped into the hall. "Your time is up, Njiko."

He looked at Kahn. "Notify me if you think of something I can add to your case, Kahn. I'm going to look into his right to speed through these cases as he has chosen to do." He left the four prisoners in their eight-by-eight space to await their fate.

*****

Eli found Frances, Judah, and Becca having dinner when he walked in the door. "Well, hello. It looks like dinner is served." He joined them, then bathed Judah and put him in bed—their nightly ritual.

Exhausted, he grabbed his laptop and lay across the bed, closing his eyes until he heard the computer ding with several e-mails. His eyes flew open as he grabbed his Mac. Bringing the screen up, he saw an e-mail from his boss, one from the missionaries that would replace him, and one from LivRocks. *Olivia.* He opened it and read it four times. She missed him. That was the best news he'd heard all day. After reading the other e-mails, he went to sleep with a smile on his face.

As the sun painted the sky a variety of hues, Eli was at his computer, writing to Olivia.

LivRocks—great e-mail address!

Hello, Olivia,

I was happy when I got your e-mail. I'm glad you're in America safely.

Since you left me weeping at the port, I've built shipping crates and started packing them, Jessicah passed peacefully, we had a beautiful service for her, Aga Kahn's trial has begun...and I've missed you every moment. I look forward to your next e-mail.

Eli

PS: I miss your smile.

CHAPTER 14

Greetings, Eli,

How did you have time to miss me when you're accomplishing so much?

I'm so sorry about Jessicah. What will happen to her baby girl?

I'm keeping this short. I don't trust my words when I'm in jet lag. I'm home safe and headed to bed for twelve hours, then I'll go see my dad.

I'm still missing you.

Olivia

*****

The courtroom was crowded, with standing-room only. Eli removed his sports jacket as the temperature rose. The judge's robe and wig had to be stifling—the price he paid to hold his position.

Detective Debano squeezed in beside him. "Are you ready for this, Eli?"

"Yes, but I'm not comfortable sending someone to the gallows that doesn't know the Lord." Eli took a deep breath and sighed.

"I think you could talk to Kahn for a hundred years and he'd never budge." The detective pointed to the side door. "I think we might start on time. They're bringing in the prisoners early today."

At twelve noon sharp, the bailiff stood at attention in the front of the room. "All rise."

Judge Sayo entered, then motioned for everyone to take a seat.

With a bang of his gavel, the room silenced, awaiting his rulings. The judge scanned the courtroom, his gaze stopping on the four men whose futures were in jeopardy. "I've spent two days unraveling the evidence that has been presented by both sides in all four cases that are before us today. I've read the confessions of you three men employed by Aga Kahn. I've examined every detail and every photo. After much contemplation, I have reached my decisions. Would our four defendants, Usama Nuthu, Zubair Walimu, Aga Kahn, and Fahad Moi, please rise?"

The scraping of wood against wood broke the silence when their chairs were shoved back as they stood with their lawyer, Njiko.

"Usama Nuthu, your loyalty to Kahn is commendable, but you should have said no when he told you to murder Joy Deckland. Therefore, I find you guilty of the premeditated murder of the missionary Joy Deckland. Before the end of the month, you will hang by the neck until dead." Judge Sayo closed a file and set it aside.

Usama slumped into his chair, put his face in his hands, and wept openly.

The judge banged his gavel. "Quiet!"

The bailiff stood and stepped toward Usama.

Judge Sayo opened another file and faced Zubair. "Zubair Walimu, to say you were 'following orders' is no excuse for placing another person's life in peril, especially the life of an innocent child. After reviewing the evidence, I find you guilty of the attempted murder of Judah Deckland and guilty of the kidnapping of Olivia Stone. You will spend the rest of your life in prison, beginning immediately." The judge slapped his folder closed.

"Aga Kahn, do something! You said Allah would be pleased!" Zubair reached for Kahn as he pleaded.

Judge Sayo banged his gavel. "Order in the court!"

Zubair sobbed as he slumped into his chair.

The judge opened the third folder. "Fahad Moi, it is sad that you chose to pledge your loyalty to Aga Kahn. I see your fingerprints in the orchestration of several crimes, such as breaking and entering at two of Zanzibar's prestigious resorts. It is apparent that when you followed Aga Kahn's orders, you broke our laws. After many long hours with the evidence presented, I find you guilty of kidnapping. If the plan had not been thwarted, you would have participated in a premeditated murder. With your pattern of criminal activity, whether directly or indirectly, you will spend twenty years in prison, beginning immediately." Judge Sayo stacked Fahad's folder with the others.

Fahad's wife cried out, then fell to the floor, sobbing.

"No, Judge! Have mercy on me! I have a family!" Fahad was desperate.

"You should have thought about them before you destroyed your future." He banged his gavel. "Order in the court! Bailiff, if the woman cannot quiet herself, she needs to be removed."

The judge took a deep breath and blew it out in a huff, then opened the last folder. He paused as the wails of the woman faded when the doors closed behind her. "Aga Kahn, your list of crimes angers me. Do you have anything to say before I pass sentencing upon you?"

"Judge, there isn't a shred of evidence that proves I committed any serious crimes. The future of Islam on this island was my foremost concern, as I'm sure it is yours. I trust that you keep my ultimate devotion to Allah in your thoughts as you continue, Your Honor." Aga Kahn attempted a smile as he nodded toward the judge.

"Good try, Kahn. But devotion to your god does not permit you to commit crimes." The judge stared at Kahn, then looked at the file before him. "Aga Kahn, I find you guilty of the murder of Joy Deckland, guilty of arson and destruction of church property at the Christian church, and I find you guilty of stalking and ordering a breaking and entering. I add a guilty verdict of attempted murder of Olivia Stone. I find you guilty of attempted murder of Judah Deckland, and guilty of kidnapping Olivia Stone. In light of these serious crimes, I sentence you to death by hanging by the end of the month."

Aga Kahn fell into his chair, stunned.

The crowd roared. Some people cried. Some applauded.

"Order in the court!" Judge Sayo banged his gavel. "Quiet! Bailiff, escort the prisoners out of my courtroom."

The noise decreased to a dull roar.

He banged his gavel again. "This court is dismissed." He stood and left.

Eli couldn't move. Debano's jaw dropped. "I've never seen a case end this quickly, especially in Africa. We did our job stacking the evidence, but this is shocking."

The courtroom emptied quickly.

Eli said his goodbyes and walked out of the building just in time to see the police car go by. He locked eyes with Aga

Kahn. Eli put his hands together as if praying, then pointed to Kahn, sending a message one more time.

*****

All hospitals smelled of antiseptic and cleaning supplies. The first whiff transported Olivia to the difficult days before her mother passed. Taking a deep breath, she pasted on a smile and entered the hospital arm in arm with her dad.

"Liv, I'm glad you're here. This is a tough one." John Stone patted his daughter's hand. "Not exactly on my bucket list."

"You're strong, and you'll come through this and be back on the golf course before you know it." She smiled in his direction.

"I pray you are right."

A nurse approached them with a wheelchair. "Mr. Stone, if you'll have a seat, we'll get you upstairs. Your daughter can join us on the fifth floor once she parks her car."

"I'll be right behind you, Dad." She turned as the nurse was confirming his birth date and putting a wristband on him.

With the car taken care of, Olivia followed the signs to the cardiac unit and found her father.

"I hate these hospital gowns." He pulled the cloth to cover his legs.

"Mom would tell you that's why they call it ICU."

He smiled. "She never lost her sense of humor."

"You two laughed a lot." Olivia sensed him getting nervous. She kept the stories coming. "Remember when she threw you a surprise fiftieth birthday party?"

"When I turned forty-nine." He laughed.

"She knew she couldn't pull it off if she waited a year, so she jumped the gun, as she called it. And remember when she wrapped books, bricks, and pieces of wood and put them under the Christmas tree, then made us search for our gifts like a scavenger hunt?"

"I think that one backfired on her when she forgot where some of the gifts were and we didn't find all of them until we moved."

Olivia laughed. "But by that time, I was learning to drive and not interested in Barbies anymore."

"She told me the reason she married me was so she could annoy me every day." He smiled. "And she did."

A different nurse entered, followed by the anesthesiologist, a lab tech, and his cardiologist, who turned to Olivia. "You must be John's beautiful daughter who flies around the world."

Olivia smiled and shook his hand. "I don't know what he's told you, but yes, I'm his daughter. Are you doing his surgery?"

"Yes. I'm Dr. Chang, and your father is going to be fine. The surgery will take about five hours. We will keep you updated on his progress using the phone in the waiting room."

While the physician talked with Olivia, the staff helped her dad onto the table, checked his vitals, attached oxygen, and inserted an IV. Another nurse waited by the door with a basin and razor to shave his chest.

"We'll be taking him back soon. Why don't you speak to him and then wait in the cardiac waiting room?" The physician moved to John's bedside. "I'll see you in there. Don't worry, you're going to be fine, and I'm good at what I do." He smiled and left the room.

Olivia moved to his bed and took her father's hand. "Dad, I'll be in the waiting room on this floor. Love you."

"I love you too, Liv." He squeezed her hand, then let go.

Olivia stopped at the door, looked back, and waved when she saw he was watching her leave. Her teary eyes blurred the signs directing her to the waiting room.

"It's this way, Olivia."

"Aunt Jana. Thanks for coming." She hugged her.

"It's going to be a long day, and you don't need to spend it alone." She led Olivia into a nice waiting room with recliners for family members, large televisions on two walls, and a coffee station with a Keurig for guests to use.

Olivia's mind went back to the small hospital in Zanzibar, and to Eli. The comparison was night and day.

"I claimed these two recliners for us and brought breakfast."

"You're the best." Olivia enjoyed her breakfast burrito, then powered up her laptop to answer e-mails. "I brought some work to pass the time. My e-mails stacked up while I was out of town." Writing Eli was pressing her.

"Don't worry about me. A friend of mine is a writer, and I'm reading her latest novel." Jana lifted the footrest on her recliner and opened her book.

Olivia looked at her aunt. "Thanks."

Jana smiled. "You're welcome."

*****

"Frances, the missionaries coming to take my place will arrive in about two weeks. That means we need to pack our suitcases and move to the guesthouse by the end of the week. I need to have this house painted before they arrive."

She was washing dishes while Judah and Becca had their morning naps. She dried her hands and faced her boss. "Are you going to be selling the furnishings?"

"No. They want to buy the appliances and basic furniture, which makes life much easier for me and them."

"Do I leave the linens, Bwana?"

"Let's leave one set for each bed, a few towels in each bathroom, and the kitchen towels. Pack the rest with your things. You can have them." He took a cold bottle of water from the refrigerator.

"Thank you, Bwana. I can do that. I will bring the suitcases in from storage for you."

"Frances, are you ready to move to Nairobi?" He leaned against the doorframe.

"I miss my family, but you and the babies are in my heart too. It is like elastic."

Eli understood her words. "New chapters are both good and bad sometimes, like elastic, tight when things are good and stretched out when things are not so good."

"I know you understand, Bwana." She went to retrieve the luggage.

Once their suitcases were packed, it didn't take long to have most of the house boxed and ready.

"Bwana, can you buy some things for Becca? She needs clothes and diapers for the trip, and a new blanket. I'm using Judah's bottles and cloth diapers now, but you will want the other kind of diapers for the trip."

"Sure. Make a list for me of things Judah and Becca need and I'll get what they need. I'll be in town tomorrow, buying paint. Do you have a suitcase for your things, Frances?"

"Yes, but Becca does not. And you need a bag for her things on the plane."

"A diaper bag?"

"Yes, that is what you call it." She turned to check on Judah, who was waking up. "Does my boy want a snack?"

As the realization of taking care of a toddler and a baby on the long plane flights hit him, he rubbed the back of his neck. "I hope they're good on the flights, Frances."

But she didn't hear his words over Judah's jabbering.

*****

Olivia jerked when the phone rang in the cardiac waiting room. She reached to answer it. "Hello."

"Is this Olivia Stone?"

"Yes, it is."

"I'm Esther Ponds, the nurse assisting with your father's surgery. Dr. Chang asked me to give you an update. Your father is doing well, his vital signs are stable, and the surgery is proceeding as expected. He estimates the procedure to take another three hours. Feel free to go get you some lunch. I have your cell phone number if we need to contact you."

"Thank you for the update." She put the receiver back on the phone and turned to Jana. "He's is doing good, and his vitals are stable. They said to get some lunch. He'll be in surgery for at least three more hours."

Jana started organizing her things. "There are four restaurants and the hospital cafeteria on the ground floor. "Let's go."

"I'm with you."

Her aunt left a jacket and an afghan on their recliners, saving their spot. Olivia smiled and shook her head as she followed the leader, her formidable aunt.

*****

Olivia,

I'm glad you're home safe and able to be with your dad during his surgery. I'm praying for his recovery.

Olivia, Aga Kahn was sentenced to hang for his crimes. The man who killed Joy will also be hung. The other two men will serve time for their part in the kidnapping and Judah's illness. I have mixed feelings about their fates. I hate to see anyone die without Jesus, but now Christianity can spread unhindered. I knew you would want to know the outcome of the trial.

Are you resting without nightmares? Are the bad experiences in Zanzibar haunting you? I pray for peace to surround you and for your father to do well with his surgery.

Frances and I are busy packing boxes and suitcases. We will move to a guesthouse soon so I can have the house painted for the new missionaries. Wi-Fi may be sketchy from time to time. I'll still be writing to you, but sending may be sporadic.

I miss you, Olivia.

Eli

PS: I have petals in my pocket...

*****

After six long hours, Dr. Chang walked into the cardiac waiting room.

Olivia stood.

"John is a strong man. He made it through the surgery fine with no glitches. We did a triple bypass. His age and overall good health are in his favor for a complete recovery. In fact, his strength after rehab will be much improved. He is in the cardiac care unit, CCU, for tonight. You can see him in about an hour. The nurse will call when you can go back there. Any questions?"

"No, I think you've answered everything for me."

Jana stood beside Olivia. "How long will he need to be in the hospital?"

"Probably a day, maybe two in CCU, then we will move him to a room in the cardiac unit on this floor. The length of his stay will be determined by how he progresses with eating, getting up and down, and walking." The doctor waited for more questions.

"Thank you for the update, Doctor, and for everything you've done for him." Olivia shook his hand.

"You're welcome, Ms. Stone." He turned and left.

Olivia breathed a sigh of relief and relaxed in the recliner. "Thank the Lord."

Jana got comfortable beside her. "Your dad is too stubborn to give up. He's never given up on anything except when your mom passed and he couldn't save her. It broke something inside him, and he withdrew into that shell of his to deal with it."

"Without me," Olivia said. "This is the first time he let me in since she died. Maybe this will be a turning point for us. That's my prayer, anyway." Jana squeezed Olivia's hand.

*****

Eli,

My dad came through the surgery well. It was a triple bypass. I haven't seen him yet. The doctor thinks he will be in the hospital for at least five days.

I'm glad the trial is over and their crime spree will end. I understand your missionary heart hurting when those without the Lord die. But heaven can now be populated with Muslims coming to the faith.

I'm not having nightmares, but Jocelyn thinks I may have some PTSD symptoms, and is arranging some counseling appointments for me.

I know you're busy, but take time to play cars with Judah.

Missing you,
Olivia

*****

"Ms. Stone, I'm Amanda, your father's nurse. You can see him now. If you'll follow me, I will take you to where he is." The nurse waited for her.

"Can my aunt come with me?"

"Yes, but only two visitors are allowed at one time."

Olivia turned to her aunt. "You want to see him?"

"I do, but you go first. I'll wait here with our things. It's you he wants to see when he wakes up."

"Okay." Olivia followed the nurse through two sets of double doors and into a room with glass observation windows. Monitors beeped. Wires went from his body to different machines. The blood pressure device inflated automatically. The nurse turned to Olivia before she reached her father.

"Do not be alarmed. He looks a lot better than most of our heart patients. There are monitors, an IV, oxygen, and an automatic blood pressure cuff, and we're monitoring his oxygen level. He is a bit swollen and pale, but that is completely normal. There could be some blood on his gown, but we will change that."

"Thank you for warning me. How long can I stay?"

"If he is awake, fifteen minutes is allowed. We don't want to tire him. But if he's sleeping, you can stay until he wakes. I will be in and out and will help you know when you should leave."

"Okay." Olivia stepped farther into the area. His eyes were open. She stepped close. "Dad, the doctor said the surgery was successful. You're going to be okay." She slipped her hand into his.

He barely squeezed her hand. "Liv, glad you're here."

"I'm glad too, Dad."

He licked his lips.

"Are you thirsty?"

"Yes."

Olivia went to find the nurse. "Amanda, he said he's thirsty. Can he have anything?"

"Wipe his lips with a cool cloth. I'll get some shaved ice. You can spoon-feed small pieces to him."

Olivia did as the nurse instructed.

"Thanks." He let his head fall back on the pillow.

"Is that better?"

"Much better."

"Are you in pain, Dad?" She put the cup on the table by his bed and leaned close.

"No, just tired."

"You rest now. Sleep all you want. Aunt Jana is with me, and your employees, our pastor, and many of your friends have been wanting an update. You're pretty popular. I'll be back during visiting hours, and I'm in constant contact with your nurse."

"Okay." His eyes closed in slumber.

Olivia watched the monitors for a few moments before she slipped out of the room.

His nurse was coming in with an injection to add to his IV.

"I'll come back during visiting hours with my aunt. He's sleeping now. If anything changes, please call my cell."

"I will. I'm keeping a close eye on him. Relax. He is doing great."

"Thank you, Amanda."

Olivia updated Jana on her visit, then created a text she sent to eleven people who were waiting to spread the word of his condition. She included Jocelyn and Ellie in those receiving the update.

"By the texts you've been receiving, he's got a lot of people who care about him," Jana said.

"Yes, he does, but I've got key people spreading the word so this list isn't a hundred people. I just hope all these people aren't planning to visit him when he gets into a room or gets home."

"That's where I come in. You can't hurt their feelings, but I can give time limits and keep things under control like a WAC sergeant, and they'll still love me when they leave. It's what I do."

"You will have time to cook too, won't you?" Olivia asked.

"Absolutely, all your favorites."

"Perfect." She smiled.

*****

"Da-da. Da-da."

Eli heard Judah calling him and crying. He was up and out of his bedroom in no time. "Judah, Daddy's coming." He hurried to his son's room. "What's the matter?" He knelt by his bed.

"Nack, Daddy, nack"

"You're hungry? Well, let's get you something to eat." He held his hands out, and Judah jumped into his arms. Eli hugged his son as they walked through the living room.

He saw the clock. "No wonder you're hungry. It's after eight o'clock. How did I sleep so late? Where's Frances? She's always here by seven thirty."

Eli got Judah a cup of cereal and carried him piggyback to check on Frances. He knocked on her door.

"Frances, are you okay." He listened for her to reply.

"Come in, Bwana."

He opened the door and found her still in bed, trembling with fever.

"Frances, you're sick. Stay in bed." He went to Jessicah's room and got her blanket to add to Frances's bed. "I will call the doctor, Frances. What does Becca need?"

"She had a bottle at four this morning. She will wake by nine and need to be changed and will want another bottle."

"Do I mix it like we did Judah's?"

"Yes, Bwana. And burp her when she finishes half the bottle."

"Okay. I've got this. I'll go call the doctor, then come back for Becca. You rest. I'll hurry."

"Sorry, Bwana."

"Not your fault, Frances. Do not worry."

He picked up Judah and went to make the call.

"Well, Judah, looks like it's you and me today. And baby Becca."

He cooked breakfast and ate with Judah, then moved Becca and her belongings into the main house while the doctor was with Frances.

"It's malaria, Bwana. I've given her medicine and left tablets by her bed. Her case isn't severe, but she will need to rest for three or four days. When her fever breaks, she will feel better and try to return to work, but make her rest another day or two so she will not relapse." He took his stethoscope from around his neck and put it in his black bag.

"I will make sure she gets the rest she needs. We will be moving to a guesthouse day after tomorrow. But we will take good care of her. Thank you for making house calls for us."

After paying the doctor and seeing him out, Eli warmed the filtered water for Becca's bottle. Judah knocked over a stack of his boards and clapped his hands.

Eli looked around at the mess Judah had made. "I think it's time to call in reinforcements, buddy."

Some faithful church members helped with meals, babysitting, and moving them to the guesthouse—a blessing for years of ministry.

*****

Eli's cell phone vibrated in his pocket as he pulled through the gates to the mission compound. "Hello, Debano. You want me to do all your work for you, right?"

The detective laughed. "Absolutely. Hey, I'm glad I caught you before you left the island."

Eli got out of his vehicle and pocketed his keys. "What's up?"

"Usama Nuthu is dead. He was smothered in his jail cell."

Eli took a sack of paintbrushes out of the truck. "So Aga Kahn punished him for his disloyalty?"

"That's my take on it. I think he has threatened the other prisoners into silence, because no one is talking."

"Will there be repercussions for his death?"

"I doubt it at this point, since he was sentenced to death by hanging. I just thought you'd want to know."

Eli could hear sirens in the distance. "I appreciate you keeping me informed about Usama, but I'm not surprised. Aga Kahn was livid he'd told all their devious secrets that sealed their fates."

"I'm relieved the case is closed. Have a safe trip, Deckland. And you're welcome back to Zanzibar anytime."

"Thanks, Detective. Maybe someday."

*****

By the end of his second day in CCU, John Stone was moved to intermediate care on the same floor. The nurses had him up for a slow walk in the hall.

"Who's Eli?" Jana watched Olivia's face. Gauging her response.

"He's a man I met in Zanzibar. Why do you ask?"

"You talk in your sleep. You called him your hero. So what's the story?"

Olivia looked at the door, then back at her aunt. "I can talk about Eli, but not about everything that happened in Zanzibar, in front of Dad. I'll tell you when we're alone."

"Are you okay, Olivia?" Jana put her hand on Olivia's arm.

"I am now. I'm going to get some counseling." She smiled. "But Eli is amazing."

*****

Hello, Olivia,

I pray your father is improving. I have my church praying for a quick recovery.

Things are ramping up here. We're in the guesthouse now while the mission house is being painted. And Frances has malaria. It's not a critical case, but she is in bed for the week. My church members have helped with meals and moving.

By the way, Happy asked me to tell you hello.

When we moved the furniture, I found six of Judah's trucks we had lost. Now he's in matchbox heaven.

There are two phone numbers at the bottom of your e-mails. Which one is your cell phone number? In case I want to call you.

I miss you more with each passing day!

Eli

CHAPTER 15

"You ready, Dad?"

"Yes, I can't wait to get home."

"We have a hospital bed set up in the den with a great view of the golf course and your perfectly manicured yard. I knew that would make you happy."

"Can't I sleep in my bed?"

"Not for a few weeks Dad. Too many stairs."

"Well, let's get going." He held up his feet so Olivia could put the footrests down on his wheelchair.

"Is Jana already at the house?"

"Yep, cooking lunch."

"Great! We will eat good, and she'll keep the vultures at bay."

"What vultures, Dad?" Olivia's brow furrowed. She rubbed between her eyebrows, remembering Eli's touch.

"Men who are chomping at the bits to take over the company if I don't pull through this."

"But it's your company. How can they do that?" Olivia hung his bag of belongings on the wheelchair.

"By buying up stock until they own more of it than I do. I should have kept a closer eye on it. But I trusted them."

"And the stress of it finally caught up with you. Now I get the picture." Olivia let Nurse Amanda commandeer the wheelchair as she rushed ahead and punched the Down button on the elevator, her mind spinning with a plan. *It's time to buy more stock.*

*****

Ticking things off his list brought Eli steps closer to seeing Olivia again. The house was painted, Frances was feeling better, and Becca's passport had arrived. Standing at the port as the palm trees danced in the brine-filled breeze, Eli waited for the ferry. The setting took Eli's thoughts back to the day Olivia arrived in Zanzibar. Her profile and stance were identical to Joy's. But her face was all Olivia. Those long eyelashes and perfect smile captivated him from the start. He turned and shaded his eyes with his hand when he heard the ferry's whistle. It was a higher-pitched sound than a tugboat working the rivers in America but always excited the children and sent birds into flight with its piercing sound.

Among the dark-skinned passengers, a family of Americans stood out like the glow worms in his flower bed. He needed no introduction.

"My guess is, you're the Poole family. The new missionaries in Zanzibar."

The man stepped off the gangplank and stuck his hand out. "Yes. I'm Jeremy Poole. This is my wife, Nina, and our sons, Derrick and Landon."

"Hello, Nina, Derrick, and Landon. Welcome to Zanzibar! It is a great place to spread the gospel in an exotic setting. You will be happy here."

"Hello, Eli. Thanks for meeting us." Jeremy pulled a suitcase and juggled two backpacks.

"My pleasure. I've hired a van to help get your things to the mission house." Eli relieved him of the two backpacks.

"That's kind of you. Apparently, you've done this before." He shook hands with Eli.

"I have. You ready to get loaded?" Eli punched the key fob for his SUV to open the luggage area.

"We're more than ready."

It took Eli's SUV and a fully loaded van to get them and their belongings to their home. Luggage and passengers jostled over potholed roads to the mission compound. As the gate guard and the van driver unloaded their luggage, Eli showed them around.

"We've left one set of clean linens for the beds and a few things in the kitchen to help get you started. The church members have brought fruits, vegetables, and bread for you as you get settled."

"That's kind of them." Nina looked through groceries.

"Jeremy, can I come by in the morning to take you to see the church property?" Eli asked as he stepped toward the door.

"That sounds perfect."

"The gate guard on duty is a loyal Christian man, and so is the night guard. But it's up to you if you keep them. My houseworker is retiring, but there are several women in the church wanting to apply for the job."

Nina stepped into the conversation. "Thank you, Eli. The house is clean, freshly painted, and ready for us. You've gone above and beyond. I appreciate it."

"It's the least I could do. I'm glad you're here."

Eli left them to unpack. He'd been there. Excited and anxious to take on the world—well, this small part of it. *Their road will be easier than mine, thanks to Joy's sacrifice.*

*****

Dear Eli,

Thanks for praying for my father. We got to bring him home today, two days earlier than expected. We have set up a hospital bed for him in our den, and my aunt is controlling that situation, monitoring visitors, and keeping us fed.

I've had a few business issues to take care of this morning but have been staying at my dad's bedside most of the time.

I've been going through my photos of my time on the island, my time with you. I have a lot of special memories... great ones. Have you ever considered being a tour guide? LOL!

The first number listed in my information is my cell; the other number is a landline that Jocelyn and Ellie use when they need to fax a grant or an article.

I've prayed for Frances. I know you're busy. Do not forget to think about us.

Liv

*****

Eli calculated the time difference between Zanzibar and Texas, then pressed in the number of Olivia's home phone.

On the third ring, he heard a groggy, "Hello."

"This is Eli Deckland. I know Olivia isn't there, but I need help with something."

"This is Jocelyn. Sorry for the slow greeting, but I just got home and had fallen asleep. I've heard a lot about you and Judah, Eli. You said you need help?"

"Yes. I'm booking my flights to come back to the States, and I want to be on Olivia's next flight. I know she works first class. But I'll be in the cheap seats. I want to surprise her with a marriage proposal during the flight. Can you help me?"

Jocelyn laughed. "Absolutely! I will call her and try to determine when she'll start working flights again. I've got a pen. Give me your e-mail address and I'll send you the information within the next few days."

"I appreciate that." He gave her his info.

"Glad to help, but if you break her heart, I'll rearrange your face."

Eli laughed out loud. "Thanks, Jocelyn. Bye."

*****

Olivia was taking her dad's food tray to the kitchen. "You want some coffee? Or do you want to rest?"

"How about some coffee and pie later?"

"You got it." Olivia walked toward the kitchen. Her cell phone buzzed in her pocket. She put the tray on the cabinet and answered.

"Hey, Jocelyn. What's up?" Olivia leaned forward and put her elbows on the granite counter to talk.

"First, how is your dad doing?"

"He is doing great. Still weak, but ahead of schedule, according to the doctors. Are you and Ellie okay?"

"Yep. Except for jet lag, we're good. Hey, do you have any idea when you can get back in the flight rotation? Your substitute is a snob."

"Well, I wouldn't want you to be tormented by a snob. Let me talk with my aunt and see when we are taking Dad to the doctor, and I'll get back to you."

"I'm glad he's doing good. I'm sure he has enjoyed the time with you."

"It has been good for us. I'll text you later today." Olivia moved toward the sink, ready to clean the lunch tray.

"Sure thing. Bye."

Olivia pocketed her phone and started putting dishes into the dishwasher.

"I overheard your conversation." Jana held up the discharge papers from the hospital. "His doctor's appointment is next Tuesday, the twenty-second. I'm planning to stay at least two weeks after that. You can go back to work after we see his doctor, if you want."

Olivia smiled. "Well, aren't you the one in the know! I'll run it by Dad, then text Jocelyn."

*****

"This plot of land was donated by the government as a burial place for David Livingstone and any Christians who died on the island. The Anglican Church gave it to us. They were tired of the upkeep and maintenance. This particular church was started after the first Christian crusade on the island. You may need to increase the size of the building to hold the growing crowd." Eli scanned the property with purpose, memorizing it.

"That sounds like a good problem to me." Jeremy smiled, excited about the challenge.

"Yes, it is." He unlocked the wooden building and stepped inside. "There are some wonderful people in this congregation. You have to keep things simple. They aren't acquainted with the Bible stories we've grown up learning."

"I can tell you love these people, Eli. I hear your heart."

"I do, and you will too." Eli stood behind the wooden pulpit on the platform built of blocks and wood.

"I think I'm stepping into a big pair of shoes."

Eli paused, collecting himself. "I'll introduce you and your family to the church on Sunday morning. There will be a dinner after church, where they will welcome you and give us gifts as they bid me farewell. During that ceremony, I'll give you my keys to the church."

"How much longer will you be here, Eli?" Jeremy followed him out of the church.

"I'm booking our tickets in the next few days, so probably a week. I'll let you know. Hey, why don't we pick up your wife and kids and go get a pizza? But I warn you, it's not Pizza Hut."

"Sounds great."

*****

Eli,

This is from Jocelyn.

Olivia will be on the flight number 1447 from Nairobi to New York on the twenty-sixth. You may want to request seats by the bulkhead since you have a young boy. Most travelers with babies and toddlers sit there.

Let me know if I can help you
further.

Jocelyn

*****

"John, you look good! We'll get those staples out of your chest before you leave the office today. I want you to continue to take it easy for a couple more weeks. That means frequent naps, no lifting, and no stress." Dr. Chang took a seat since he had completed his assessment of his patient.

"What about the stairs?" John asked. "My bedroom is on the second floor."

"Take them slowly. Stop and rest if you get winded."

"I'll do that."

"We'll make sure he does, Doctor." Olivia smiled. "What about work? It's stressful, and I don't want him to overdo it."

"John, don't return to the office until I see you again in two weeks. Then we'll talk."

"Olivia will be going back to work, but my sister will be with me until my next appointment. If I'm good, can I go back for half-days?" John pressed for answers.

"Barring any new developments, yes." Dr. Chang stood and put John's chart under his arm.

Olivia loved the smile that spread across her dad's face.

"I'll send someone in to remove those staples. It's good to see you doing so well." He stepped closer, put his hand on John's shoulder, and left the room.

"That's great news, Dad. Why don't you lie back on these two pillows until she gets the staples out?"

"I couldn't have done this without you, Liv."

"I'm glad I could help." She paused. "Dad, I've done something you might need to know about." She gave him a small smile.

"What's that?"

She had his attention. "I bought some more stock in your company. A lot. And I hold the majority of the stock. Your opposition doesn't know it yet, but they have lost their power." Olivia grinned.

"How did you do that?"

"I made a few calls to your old friends Pennington, Collins, and Walkers and talked them into selling their stock to me. I explained the stress of the situation you were in, and they were happy to help. And don't worry, they made a great profit. When you add that stock to what I already own, I hold the power in my hands."

"Liv, why would you do that?" He took her hand.

"I love you, Dad. If I can use some of my inheritance from Grandmother's estate to relieve the pressure you're under, it seemed like the perfect gift I could give you."

"I don't have words, Olivia. I can truly relax now." He teared up. "I appreciate what you've done."

"Just let me know what they say when they discover the shift in power. I'd love to be a fly on the wall." She squeezed his hand.

*****

Eli,

I haven't received an e-mail from you, so you must be without Wi-Fi.

My dad got a great report from the doctor today. A few more weeks of rest and he will start working half-days at the office. That means I'll be going back to work soon.

I'm glad Frances is feeling better. She is a sweet lady. I'm sure you and Judah are going to miss her when she goes to live with her family.

Missing people you care about has taken on a new meaning for me since I left you at the port of Zanzibar. It made my heart hurt.

Still does.

Olivia

*****

"So tell me about Eli." John Stone hung on as Olivia turned onto the road in front of the hospital.

"You heard me and Aunt Jana talking. I thought you were asleep."

"I faked it."

She took the entrance ramp to the interstate. "You're bad."

"Is he a good man, Liv?"

"He's the best, Dad. He is a missionary, a widower. He's an attractive man of integrity. He's courageous and strong and kind."

"And he has won your heart."

"Yes. But I'm not what he needs. He has an adorable son, but he will want more children that I can't give him. And on top of that, I'm not a missionary."

"He lives in Zanzibar?" he asked.

"Yes, but he's moving home soon." She looked at him while waiting for a red light to change.

"Where's home for him?"

"Katy, Texas." She smirked.

"Katy, then what's the problem? That's only a few miles down the road."

"I'm guarding my heart—that's the problem. What if he realizes he needs to find a missionary to spend his life with? It was a quick romance with a lot of interruptions. How can you be sure in such a short time?"

"Olivia, you know your heart. You're just focusing on the what-ifs too much. Pray about it and trust the Lord. He hasn't failed you yet." He spoke wisdom.

"No, He hasn't." She pulled into the circle drive in front of his huge brick home in the Woodlands, a suburb of Houston. "Let's get you inside. You can have some lunch, then take a slow walk upstairs."

"That sounds like a win to me."

She released her seat belt, then hurried around to open his door.

He stood and caught her gaze. "Give love a chance, Liv."

"That's what he said."

*****

Eli stopped to check on the Pooles. "Hello in the house."

Nina was in the kitchen. "Come in, Eli. I'll get Jeremy. He's out back in the yard with the boys."

Jeremy came through the back door with two dirty boys on his heels. "You two get cleaned up before you get dirt all over the floors."

"Hey, Eli."

"Are you guys settling in okay? Do you need anything?" He stuffed his hands into the front pockets of his jeans and stood by the front door.

"We're good. Almost unpacked and getting organized. How are you doing?" Jeremy went to the kitchen sink and washed his hands.

"I'm good. I've booked our tickets. We leave in two days." Eli leaned against the doorframe.

"Are you ready for the move? You're making big changes, my friend."

"Yeah, it's time. I need to get my family home, and I have someone waiting for me. That makes it easier. On another subject, I'll get the SUV serviced in the morning, then can I bring it to you? I'll need a lift back to the guesthouse."

"Sure. Do you need help getting to the port?" Jeremy dried his hands and leaned against the kitchen cabinet.

"No. I've hired a large van to get us there, but thanks."

"Thanks for all you've done to make this transition easy for us. We appreciate it. And the welcome we received at the church was amazing. You were right. They are great people."

"Yes, they are. After I'm gone, feel free to e-mail me with questions as you begin to move about the island and start your ministry."

"What would you do first, if you were me?" Jeremy asked.

Eli thought for a minute. "I'd see the sights, take some tours, and visit the beach. It will help you to know the good about your area, your mission field, before you begin facing issues and get busy with ministry."

"That sounds like wisdom to me, and it will make the boys happy."

"See you tomorrow." Eli turned and took the steps off the front porch. When he got to his SUV, he stood and looked at the house for a minute. He would miss this place.

*****

Jocelyn,

I've booked our tickets, and we are on her flight in the coach section at the back of the plane, by the bulkhead, as you suggested. Our seat assignment is 56A and 56B.

I need help!

I don't want Olivia to see us board the plane. I'd like to surprise her at some point during the flight. Can you make that happen?

Please give me instructions.

Thanks,
Eli Deckland

*****

Wearing shorts and a T-shirt, Olivia pulled her suitcase to the front door, then took the stairs to her dad's bedroom. "Hi, Dad. How are you feeling today?" She sat on a chair by his bed and tied the laces on her sandals, which wrapped around her ankles, remembering the wounds she'd endured and the hunky hero that came to her rescue.

"I'm good. I got my shower, and I'm moving slow but feeling stronger every day."

"How's it feel to be back in your own bed?"

"Wonderful." He sat up a little. "Liv, I love the chess set. It's the best one I've ever seen. Thanks."

"Eli picked it out. It was carved by a local artisan in Zanzibar." She stood. "I'm packed, and I need to pick up my uniforms at the dry cleaners on my way home. I work a flight tonight traveling to and from Nairobi again. With our Nairobi layover, the job will take us five days."

"You be careful. Love you, Liv."

"Love you too, Dad." She kissed his cheek and hurried downstairs, where her aunt was taking her things to her car.

She opened her arms for a hug. "Love you."

"You're the best, Aunt Jana Rose. Keep your eye on him."

"You know I will. Don't worry. Just be safe."

"I promise." Olivia felt a mixture of sadness and excitement as she left her dad's home. But it was time to get back to work. Time to see what the future held, whatever that was.

*****

Eli,

As flight attendants, we will board the plane first.

Once you're in the airport, don't be near the assigned gate until they start boarding first class. Olivia will have to be ready to greet passengers in her area and won't see you.

Then board with the passengers with small children. They will send you to the back entrance of the plane. Ellie will be your flight attendant. I've made her aware of your wishes, and she will help us make it happen.

I'll come to see you after all the passengers have boarded the plane.

Jocelyn

*****

While they waited at the port, Eli gave an envelope to Frances. "Here is a bonus for you for all your hard work and faithful service to my family. We love you, and I couldn't have made it without your help."

She took the envelope and put it in her purse. "Asante, Bwana. It has been a blessing to me." A tear coursed her cheek.

The whistle of the ferry excited Judah, but it made Becca cry. Frances held her close as they boarded the ferry with all their suitcases and two diaper bags. Eli watched Zanzibar diminish in the distance as the ferry took them to Tanzania. So many memories, very good and very bad, had occurred on that island. But it was time to move on.

Once they took the flight from Dar es Salaam to Nairobi, it was time to say goodbye to Frances. Eli hugged her, then took Becca into his arms. "Judah, give Frances a bye kiss." Judah kissed her. She cried.

"No cry, no cry. Love you."

"He's never said that before, Frances. He said it first to you." Eli put his arm around her shoulders. Eli gave her a photo of her holding Judah that he'd framed.

"I will cherish this, Bwana."

Her family surrounded her with hugs and kisses. As they ushered her away, she looked back and waved at Eli. He returned the wave.

Eli hired some Kenyans to help him get their pile of luggage to the British Air terminal at the other end of the international airport. After the fiasco of getting them through security and checking in for their flight, Eli took his little family to Java House, an American-owned restaurant at one end of the airport. They would have quite a wait, but he could feed Becca her bottle and let Judah play with his cars. It would keep them out of sight until they could board the Boeing 757.

*****

"Aren't we a bit early, Ellie? There's not a long line yet."

"There's some rain moving in soon, and you know I melt when it rains, and my hair frizzes. I'm ugly with frizzy hair. And…I wanted to get ahead of it so you wouldn't get your uniform wet." Ellie pulled her suitcase toward the first security check.

"Well, we're here now. We can board early and relax in first class for a bit before the passengers come aboard." Olivia pulled her luggage behind her as she followed Jocelyn to the first security check.

"Are you glad to be back working flights?" Ellie asked.

"Yes. I think getting back to my routine is helping me deal with what happened." Olivia lifted her carry-on to the security belt.

"I'm glad, because we missed you." Ellie smiled and retrieved her luggage from the belt. "You know, like that piece of popcorn that gets stuck in your tooth." Ellie laughed at her own joke.

"Oh, I feel loved." Olivia followed her friends through the process. They kept moving until they were on the plane.

"Coke or Sprite?" Olivia took their orders and served them as a waitress would.

"I need an update on your upcoming trip to Timbuktu, Ellie. Is it on the calendar yet?" Olivia got comfortable and slipped off her pumps.

"I may have an e-mail from the editor of the magazine when I get home. They have a French-speaking interpreter that knows the area who will accompany me." Ellie took a drink of Coke.

"I'm glad you won't be going alone." Olivia stilled.

Ellie put her hand on Olivia's. "You're going to be okay. A hero saved you, and the Lord brought you home safely."

"I know. I keep going through the motions. One day I'll get past it."

"Well, you're not alone. You've got us," Ellie said as she put her glass on Olivia's tray.

Ellie stood, then bent down to look out the plane window into the terminal. "They're starting to line up the first-class passengers, and the other flight attendants are boarding now. I better get back to the cheap seats. See you two later." She turned and retreated to her section of the huge plane.

Jocelyn slipped her feet into her shoes. "Have a good flight, Olivia. I'll chat with you later, if things don't get too crazy."

*****

When they finally called for passengers who had small children to board the plane, Eli was exhausted. Both of his babies were fussy. Filing in behind other families, he found their seats and smiled when he saw a bed they provided for Becca to sleep in. Judah loved his seat. He jumped in it a couple of times, then dumped his cars in the seat and started playing. Eli was glad to put Becca into the bed. She smiled and kicked her feet. Eli deposited his carry-on in the overhead bin and got the two diaper bags off his shoulders.

A pretty blond flight attendant stopped at his seat. She looked up at his seat number, then looked at Eli. "Are you Eli Deckland?" Ellie asked.

"I am. Are you Ellie?"

"Yes. Whose baby?"

"Mine. She's adopted."

Her eyes widened. "Does Olivia know about her?"

"No. She's a gift to Olivia if she accepts my proposal."

"What a beautiful baby! She has gorgeous blue eyes."

"Could I get a bottle warmed for her later in the flight?"

Ellie smiled. "Of course. But if I'm too busy, I'm sure the flight attendant in first class can warm it for you." She picked up a car that had fallen behind their row of seats and leaned over to Judah.

"Is this your car?" she asked Judah.

Judah nodded, then signed thank-you.

"He signed thank-you." Ellie smiled.

Judah blew her a kiss.

"Olivia has told us about you, Judah Deckland. I think I'll keep you myself." She looked at Eli again. "Let me know when you need that bottle warmed."

"I will, thanks."

"Da-da, nack."

Eli reached for his diaper bag and gave him his snack cup with goldfish crackers in it. Knowing it would make him thirsty, he put his sippy cup within reach. He gave a toy to Becca, who seemed to be happy stretching out and rolling around in the bed. She smiled at Eli. "You like the new toy I bought you, sweet girl?"

Ellie stopped at Eli's seat and handed him a cold bottle of water. "You look pretty weary. Want some cold water?"

"That would be awesome, thank you. I've never traveled alone with two little ones. But they're both good babies." He opened the bottle.

"Let me know if you need assistance." She moved on as Eli guzzled the cold water.

It took almost an hour to fill the plane and get the doors shut. After takeoff, Becca began to get fussy. Eli prepared a bottle for her and changed her diaper. He changed Judah as well, knowing it was way past his bedtime. When the Fasten Seat Belt sign was turned off, Ellie approached Eli.

"You need some help, Eli?"

"Could you watch these two for a minute while I wash my hands and get rid of these two diapers?"

"Sure."

Eli turned to Judah. "Judah, I will be right back. Can you show Ms. Ellie your cars?"

Judah grabbed his favorite truck and stepped into Eli's vacant seat. "Car."

"Yes, you like cars, Judah?"

He ran the car on the back of the seat and up Ellie's arm and laughed.

Eli returned and watched Ellie play with Judah for a minute before approaching. "He's a charmer."

"I love him already." She looked at Becca rubbing her eyes. "You need that bottle warmed?"

"Yes, I do."

Ellie smiled, took the bottle, and headed to first class.

*****

"Olivia, it's crazy back there. Can you warm a bottle for me? It belongs to the passenger in 56A." Ellie held a baby bottle toward Olivia.

"Sure. I'll bring it to you in a few minutes. I'm caught up here." Olivia turned and poured hot water into a basin and put the bottle in.

Ellie returned to coach class, stopping to update Jocelyn as she passed through business class. "J, when Olivia comes this way with a baby bottle, follow her. I'll hand you a baby girl. Feed her the bottle and watch what happens."

"Okay, you've got it. I'm excited!" Jocelyn smiled and collected some trash from a passenger.

"She'll be shocked. I've gotta get back there." Ellie hurried back to coach class, staying close to the row where Eli was seated. She gave him a thumbs-up.

Eli was playing with Judah on his lap so he would see Olivia first. Becca was fussy but lying in the bed that was attached to the bulkhead in front of Judah's seat.

When Jocelyn saw Olivia coming with the baby bottle, she followed her to coach class.

*****

Knowing Olivia would get there momentarily, Eli jostled Judah, keeping him awake so he could see Olivia.

Ellie saw Olivia coming with Jocelyn behind her. "Eli, she's coming. Showtime!"

Eli stood Judah up on his lap and turned him around.

"Mama, Mama." Judah lunged into Olivia's arms.

"Judah! My sweet boy. I'm so glad to see you!" She hugged Judah, then looked over his head and caught Eli's gaze. "Eli." She froze.

Ellie stepped up, took the bottle out of Olivia's hand, and gave it to Jocelyn. She reached over the seat and picked up Becca and handed her to Jocelyn.

"Judah, come to Ms. Ellie. I have a snack for you in my pocket." She took Judah from Olivia.

Eli stood and stepped into the aisle. "Hello, Olivia. I knew I could find you if I flew the African skies."

"You were looking for me?"

He took her hand. "Absolutely. I've missed you with every breath."

Her eyes filled with tears. "I've missed you too, Eli. So much."

"I have a question I need to ask you." He knelt in the aisle and looked up at her. "Olivia, I love you and can't live without you. Will you marry me?" He reached into his pocket and pulled out a ring box holding a sparkling oval-shaped diamond ring.

A tear coursed down her cheek. "Yes, oh, yes, I'll marry you! I love you, Eli!"

He stood, embraced her, and gave her a passionate kiss.

The passengers applauded. Judah clapped his little hands.

Eli leaned back and slipped the solitaire onto her finger and kissed her hand, then wrapped her in his embrace.

Olivia hugged him for a long moment, then leaned back with questions in her expression. "Wait. Who was the baby bottle for?"

Eli smiled and took Becca from Jocelyn. "I have a gift for you, Olivia. I adopted her. She's yours."

Tears streamed down Olivia's cheeks. "She's beautiful." She looked up at Eli. "You mean it?"

"With all my heart. Becca is yours." He put her into Olivia's arms.

Becca looked at Olivia and smiled.

Applause and whistles filled the air. Their captive audience loved the live entertainment.

"So let me get this straight. I get you and Judah and Becca when I say 'I do'?"

"That's right. It's a packaged deal." Eli grinned.

"I just have one thing to say…"

Eli waited.

Olivia looked at the passengers. "Is there a preacher on this airplane?"

Laughter erupted.

She handed Becca back to Jocelyn, then turned and kissed her fiancé passionately, with forever on her mind.

EPILOGUE

"Hamburger and fries, God bless America!" Eli dipped his last fry in his ketchup and ate it with a smile.

"So you've missed American cuisine, Mr. Missionary?" Olivia asked. "You cleared that plate in record time."

"It's one of the things we sacrifice." Eli finished his Dr. Pepper.

"So how do we do this?" Olivia, still in her flight attendant uniform, looked up from watching Becca's face as the baby fell asleep. "I mean, logistically." Seated in a booth in Five Guy's Burgers restaurant, in LaGuardia Airport in New York City, she stacked their dishes so their waitress could remove them.

"I haven't thought much past getting you to say yes. But we're all going to be in jet lag and our babies will have their days and nights mixed up. My family doesn't know about us yet, and Becca is also a surprise. Do you have any suggestions?"

She glanced at Judah. "Judah's falling asleep. Why don't you lay him on the bench before his face ends up in his plate?" Olivia pulled a wipe from the diaper bag and held it out to Eli.

Eli cleaned Judah's face and laid him down. He patted his back as he returned his focus to his fiancée.

Olivia took a drink of her tea and checked her watch. "We have about an hour before I need to get to the plane. I'm glad you're on my flight, Eli. I couldn't believe it when I saw Judah, then you."

"It was perfect. Jocelyn and Ellie have been very helpful." He reached over the table and took Olivia's hand. "I know we have a lot of details to work out, but together we can find our answers."

"I agree." She smiled and squeezed his hand. "So your family is meeting you at the Houston airport?"

"Yeah, they'll come in several vehicles because we have so much luggage. What are you thinking?"

"We can shock them, catch them totally off guard with your fiancée, who looks like your late wife, and a new baby girl you adopted—or you and Judah can go with them and I'll take Becca with me. That will give you time to prepare them."

He sat back against the vinyl of the booth. "I hadn't thought about you taking Becca. Are you sure?"

"Absolutely. I don't want to put her down." Olivia kissed the sleeping baby's forehead.

"Okay." He thought for a moment. "At baggage claim, I'll put her suitcase beside yours and give you her car seat when I retrieve Judah's. Then I'll call you later tonight, after everyone has gone to bed."

"It sounds like a plan. But when will I see you again?" She put a strand of hair behind her ear that had fallen out of the required bun flight attendants wear.

"My family's having a get-together on Saturday at noon to welcome us home. That will give me two days to bring them up-to-date. Why don't you and Becca join us?"

Olivia looked down at the sweet baby in her arms, then met Eli's gaze. "We'd love to."

*****

"Dad, Aunt Jana, where are you? I have something to show you." Olivia juggled her purse and a diaper bag while carrying Becca.

"We're in the den, Olivia." Her dad's voice seemed stronger.

Olivia, dressed in leggings and an oversized T-shirt, left her purse and the diaper bag in the foyer and entered the den with Becca.

"Welcome back! And who is this?" Aunt Jana Rose stood to embrace Olivia and to look at the baby girl. Becca was dressed in a sundress with matching sandals and headband, with a bow around her curly light-brown hair. Her bright blue eyes and chubby cheeks captivated anyone who saw her precious face.

Olivia held Becca in front of her for them to see the stunning baby girl. "This is Becca. She is half-American and half-Zanzibari. And she's mine."

"Yours? I don't understand. Wait. Is that an engagement ring on your finger?" Jana reached for her hand. "That's gorgeous, Olivia!"

Olivia grinned. "Thanks. It is a beautiful ring. This story would make a great Lifetime movie. I said yes to Eli Deckland. He adopted Becca and gave her to me."

"Wow, I think we need to hear this story! Let me hold Becca while you fill us in, Olivia." Jana took the baby, who'd started to fuss.

"She wants her bottle." Olivia got one out of her diaper bag and gave it to Jana. She stepped to her dad, who was reclining on the sofa, and kissed his cheek. "You look and sound stronger. How are you doing?"

"Much better. But enough about me. You have a tale to tell." He sat up straighter and got comfortable.

Olivia smiled, sat in a chair across from him, and filled them in on the big changes that had happened in her life.

"So I'm getting a son-in-law and a baby girl?" Her dad sat up a little straighter.

"And an adorable grandson." She showed him Judah's picture on her phone. "This is Judah. And you're going to love him."

"I'm so happy for you, Olivia. You're glowing, my dear." Her father reached for her hand. "Your mother would be thrilled!"

"She's the missing piece in this scenario."

All conversation stalled. Olivia stood and walked to the window, staring at the view.

Jana broke the stilted silence. "Well, I've been listening and enjoying this precious baby, but we have a wedding to plan, some showers to give, and some toys to buy. I need details, Olivia." She had Becca on her shoulder, trying to burp her. "My mind is spinning."

Olivia turned to face her aunt. "Becca and I will meet the family on Saturday. Eli and I haven't been able to make any plans yet. But it will be soon. Can they come to meet you two on Sunday?"

Jana looked at John, then at Olivia. "Sunday is perfect."

"How about lunch at noon with lots of macaroni and cheese and some toy cars for Judah?" Olivia asked.

"I think we can manage that." John smiled. "Jana can do the work, and I'll enjoy my grandson."

*****

Olivia was past ready to sleep, if only Becca was. After putting footie PJs on her, feeding her a warm bottle, Olivia got comfortable in the rocking chair in the corner of the condo's living room and started rocking. Becca's eyes were getting heavy.

As the back-and-forth movement threatened to put Olivia to sleep, she occupied herself thinking about the memories she would leave behind when she moved. Living with her best friends in Kingwood, Texas, had been great, but life was quickly changing. It was ingenious to live with Ellie and Jocelyn this close to the international airport. The three-bedroom, three-bath layout with a chef's kitchen worked for the threesome. They'd enjoyed living here; so much laughter filled these rooms. She'd miss them.

Her cell phone vibrated in her robe pocket. She moved her sleeping baby to grab the phone and answer Eli's call.

"Hello, Olivia." Eli sounded tired.

"Eli, it's good to hear your voice. Are you about to crash?"

"Yeah. Judah just fell asleep. My parents have kept him awake for me, so hopefully, he will sleep tonight. How's Becca?"

"I'm rocking her to sleep right now. She seems to be adjusting to the time change pretty well. My dad and aunt Jana thought she was gorgeous." Olivia kept the rocker moving as they talked.

"So you've shared our news."

"Yes, and they're ecstatic. They want to meet you and Judah. Can you two come to my dad's for lunch on Sunday?" Becca relaxed in slumber in her arms. Olivia pulled her closer to keep her arm from falling asleep.

"Absolutely! Where does he live?"

"In the Woodlands. I'll text you his address."

"You're kidding. The Woodlands? That's amazing! I had an interesting call today. A job offer at a large church in the Woodlands. I go for an interview next Tuesday."

"In a church? Are you okay working in a church after serving on the mission field? It will be totally different. Are you sure about this?" She stopped the rocking chair.

"Yes, it's a great opportunity for me, and I'm at peace with the decision. My mission director agrees. I've had too many changes happening in my life. With Judah's birth, Joy's murder, the Kahn events, you entered my life, then I adopted Becca. He thinks working stateside is best for us. We need to get established as a family."

"Is this our first step?" She covered a yawn.

"No, the first step is our wedding. I can't wait to say 'I do!'" He laughed. "Then after our honeymoon…"

"I can't wait. I love you, Eli. Marry me soon, okay?"

"Absolutely! I'm anxious to make you mine, Liv. But for now, why don't you get some rest? We will talk again tomorrow. Love you."

*****

Good morning, Olivia.

One question. When do you fly again?"

Love you,
Eli

Olivia read the text, checked on Becca, who was sleeping peaceably in a porta crib, then slipped into the kitchen still wearing her fluffy robe and slippers.

"Hey, what's up? You look deep in thought." Jocelyn stirred creamer into her coffee. "Want some caffeine?"

"Yeah, thanks." Olivia took a seat at their high-top table and stared out the window. "Eli just texted, asking me when I fly again."

"Did you answer him?" Jocelyn put a cup of coffee in front of her. "Or do you know the answer to his question?"

"Jocelyn, I've never been at this place before. I've always wanted to be a flight attendant. But lately, I've wanted to step out and do more with my life. So I went to Zanzibar, looking for my future. But jobs there are so scarce and I'd be putting the locals out of a job if I took one. So I dropped that idea. But Eli…"

"You've lost your desire to fly the skies." Ellie entered the room and dropped two pieces of bread into the toaster. "It's all over your face when you're with Eli."

"And when you hold Becca." Jocelyn took a sip of her coffee, then put her hand on Olivia's arm. "Liv, I think you found your future in Zanzibar. It's Eli, Judah, and Becca. And that's okay. In fact, it's wonderful!"

Olivia sat back in her chair. "It's time to resign, isn't it?"

Ellie took the seat next to Olivia. "Your world has changed, Liv. And now it's full of love, promise, and a chance at the future you've only dreamed about."

Tears filled Olivia's eyes. "I'm going to miss you two so much."

"Did we tell you we're starting our own B&B?" Ellie winked at Jocelyn, asking her to play along.

"Hey, I own this condo, and you two think you're starting a bed-and-breakfast?"

"No, B&B stands for bridesmaids and babysitters." They laughed. Jocelyn went to Olivia to join her and Ellie for a group hug.

*****

Good morning, Eli.

I'm so ready to see you again!
　　I don't plan to do this in the future without your input, but I've made a big decision. I'm resigning from my current job to give you and Judah and Becca my full attention. I went to Zanzibar looking for my future, and I found it—*you*!
　　Does that answer your question?

Love you,
Liv

Eli grinned. "Yes!" He pumped his fist in the air.

Judah looked up from the floor, where he was playing with the new toys Eli's family had given him. "Dada." He clapped his hands.

Eli mussed Judah's hair, then sent a text as fast as his fingers would type.

Olivia,

　　I am thrilled, to say the least. I wasn't going to ask you to give up your career to be with me. I can't find words to express what this means. I'll have to show you in person.

Love you too,
Eli

*****

270

Nerves gripped Olivia's stomach. Standing in front of the Deckland ranch-style home, she cradled Becca, with her purse and a diaper bag in tow, trying to look her best after getting lost twice. She rang the doorbell. When Eli opened the door, she wanted to cry.

"You're here. I've waited for a lifetime." He put his hands on her cheeks and kissed her softly. "Let me take Becca and the diaper bag." He relieved her of the weight she was carrying.

"A lifetime, huh?" Olivia breathed deep a couple of times, preparing to meet the future in-laws. She went up on her tiptoes and kissed Eli. "I'm so glad to see you."

He winked at her. "Everyone is anxious to meet you and Becca. So fix your lip gloss and let's do this." He touched the corner of her mouth. "Sorry, I messed it up a bit."

She made the repair, put her hand through his elbow, and walked into a small crowd of friendly faces, glad she'd worn her crinkle gauze skirt, because wrinkles didn't show.

"Mama!" Judah ran her direction with his arms in the air for her to pick him up. Tears threatened as she realized she'd come full circle. But this time she was his new mama.

Eli's mother stepped forward and put her hand on Olivia's arm. "I know who you are." She smiled.

Eli moved closer. "Mom, this is Olivia Stone, my fiancée."

"Son, the moment I saw her, I knew she's the answer to my prayers. Welcome to the family, Olivia Stone. I'm Jeanne Deckland." She hugged Olivia. "Now, who is this gorgeous baby?"

"This is Becca Deckland, your granddaughter." Eli held her toward his mother.

Jeanne moved closer. Becca touched her grandmother's face as a tear made its way down Jeanne's cheek. "Welcome, sweet baby." She took the baby from Eli and cuddled Becca, who squealed in delight.

*****

Olivia met Eli in her father's front yard. He hugged her. Judah got between them. "Mama, me up." Then he signed *please* and held his arms up.

"He said please, so I'll have to kiss you later, Eli." She picked him up and started for the front door.

"So is this how it's going to be?" He teased her and stopped in his tracks.

She pivoted and came back toward him. "You never have to worry about being slighted, Mr. Deckland. I'll make my moves after the kids are asleep." She winked and led the way into the mansion of a home.

He let out a breath that he didn't realize he'd been holding and followed her into the welcoming arms of Aunt Jana Rose and John Stone, Olivia's father.

"Eli, it's wonderful to meet you. Hello, Judah, I'm Aunt Jana. Please excuse me. I need to deal with a dirty diaper." Jana left them in the foyer.

"Dad, this is Eli Deckland, and this is Judah." She looked at Judah, then turned toward Eli. "Eli, this is my dad, John Stone."

John shook Eli's hand. "So you're the man who has won my daughter's heart?"

"Yes, sir. I love Olivia." Eli kept eye contact. "I know it's after the fact, but I'd like to ask your blessings, sir."

"We will have time to talk." John squeezed Eli's shoulder.

Olivia changed their focus. "Judah, this is Papa John. And he has some toys just for you." Judah clapped his chubby hands. "Tell him thank you, Judah." Judah signed thank-you and wiggled to get down. He reached for John's hand and waited for him to lead the way.

John looked at Eli and Olivia with tear-filled eyes. "Thank you."

Judah was in heaven with a plethora of new cars with a high-rise parking garage.

Aunt Jana was changing Becca's clothes. "Olivia, lunch will be ready in about twenty minutes. You and Eli can make yourselves comfortable."

"If you two are okay with our babies, I need to check the updates that were made at the property around the corner."

Jana picked up Becca and kissed her cheek. "We got this. Take your time."

Olivia asked Eli, "You up for a little walk?"

"Sure." He grabbed her hand and opened the front door. "Lead the way."

They walked half a block and turned up a driveway. Taking a key out of her pocket, she opened the door and stepped inside. When the door clicked shut, she turned and embraced Eli, capturing his lips, breathing in the masculine scent that was his alone. He returned her kiss and added a few of his own.

Eli leaned back but kept her in his arms. "Hi, LivRocks."

"Hello to you too." She grinned and gently touched his face. "I do have to check a few things while we're here."

"So you need me to let you go?" He held on.

"Only momentarily." She kissed him again, then headed for the kitchen with Eli close behind.

"This is a gorgeous home."

"I agree." She checked the granite work that was repaired in the kitchen, then ran her hand over the backsplash over the stove. She ticked a form the contractor left on the granite counter and signed the paper. She put the pen down, then faced Eli. "So how are you feeling about the job at the church here in the Woodlands?"

"I've talked to the pastor again since his initial offer, and I think it's a done deal. I can accept the position when I meet with him on Tuesday. How do you feel about it?"

"I trust you to make this decision. If you're at peace, then accept the offer, and I'm happy to help you any way I can. What will you be doing?"

"I'll be an assistant pastor at the main campus, and the mission pastor at all three of their campuses. It will be a challenge, but I still get to do missions."

"Then I say accept the job."

"They will love you, Liv." He ran his finger along her cheek.

"They already do." She smiled. "I grew up in that church."

He laughed. "Why didn't you say something?"

She shrugged her shoulder. "I wanted you to be able to make your decision without me in the mix. So...we're going to live in the Woodlands? That's good news."

"Is that because we'll be close to your dad?"

"Nope."

"No?" he asked.

She opened a drawer in the kitchen island and gave him a small gift-wrapped package.

"What's this?"

"A small present for you."

He pulled the ribbon off the box and lifted the lid. "It's a key." He met her eyes with a furrowed brow.

"It's a house key, to this house. I own it, and I'm giving it to you?"

He grinned. "This is yours?"

"It was. Now it's yours. Ready for a tour?"

"Absolutely."

She grabbed his hand and led him into the living room decorated with overstuffed leather furniture facing a stone fireplace with an ample hearth. Raw silk drapes added a rustic touch. The brass trunks she'd bought in Zanzibar were lined along a wall. He spied an in-ground pool in the backyard through a pair of French doors. Pivoting, he saw a baby grand piano, then started rubbing the back of his neck. "Liv, can I ask you a personal question?"

She turned to him. "Eli, you can ask me anything."

He hesitated. "Olivia, do you have money?"

She grinned, stepped up on the six-inch stone hearth, and put her arms around his neck. "Yep, I'm loaded."

Eli leaned his head back and laughed. "I think this is going to be fun!"

"I can't wait." She kissed him, then hung on, laughing as he twirled her 'round and 'round, making her dizzy from the circular motion—or was her dizziness from the whirlwind romance that landed her in the middle of her dream come true?

It was another moment to memorize…

The End

ENDNOTES

In *The Sahar of Zanzibar*, Olivia tried to choose a new path for her life. When her flawed plan fell through, her life was threatened. In desperation, she surrendered her future to the Lord. With Him directing her path, she walked a bumpy road for a while, but in the end, she was blessed beyond her wildest dreams and set upon a road to a happily ever after.

When I'm faced with a problem or a decision, I tend to try to figure it out on my own. I make a plan and execute the plan. But Proverbs 3:5–6 says, "Trust in the Lord with all thine heart and lean not on thine own understanding. In all thy ways acknowledge Him, and He will direct thy paths" (KJV). Allowing the Lord to take the reins takes faith and absolute trust. But I've learned that when He is directing my life, things work out better than I could imagine.

I pray that this truth is planted into your spirit, and by letting the Lord orchestrate your life, you are richly blessed.

Thank you for reading my debut novel.

Blessings,
Shirley

KENYA'S KIDS

Twenty-two years ago, the Lord burdened my heart concerning the urgent needs of 350,000 orphaned children roaming the streets of Kenya. These children have worms in their stomachs, lice in their hair, and fungus on their hands and feet. Their parents have died from AIDS, typhoid, and malaria, leaving them to fend for themselves. They sleep on sidewalks, in alleys, and near the garbage dumps, where they find most of their food.

We started taking children off the streets twenty years ago, and over four hundred children have called Kenya's Kids Home for Street Children their home. Lives are being transformed every day.

It is the passion of my heart, the mission to which I'm called. It's my desire for a portion of every book's profits to go to support Kenya's Kids. Thank you for your contribution.

If you would like to help me help the children, you can send a check to Finish the Task Ministries, PO Box 526, White House, TN 37188, or by giving through Venmo at Finishthe-Task, or through PayPal.

Thank you for caring about Kenya's Kids!

ABOUT THE AUTHOR

Shirley Gould is an inspirational speaker, an African missionary, and an author. She's the founder of Kenya's Kids Home
for Street Children, an orphanage in Kenya. Shirley has
written nonfiction for thirty years and is presently writing
Christian fiction novels. She lives in the Nashville, Tennessee,
area. Follow her writing journey and watch for the sequel's
release at shirleygould.org.